29/3

CANOEING

Also in the Pelham Pictorial Sports Instruction Series

John Dawes: Rugby Union
Chester Barnes: Table Tennis
Henry Cooper: Boxing
Bob Wilson: Soccer
Barry Richards: Cricket
Richard Hawkey: Squash Rackets
Ken Adwick: Golf
Jack Karnehm: Understanding Billiards and Snooker
Rachael Heyhoe Flint: Women's Hockey
Paul and Sue Whetnall: Badminton
Bill Scull: Gliding and Soaring
Denis Watts: Athletics—Jumping and Vaulting
John le Masurier and Denis Watts: Athletics—Track Events
Howard and Rosemary Payne: Athletics—Throwing
Celia Brackenridge: Women's Lacrosse
Brian Jacks: Judo
David Haller: Swimming

Pelham Pictorial Sports Instruction Series

Peter Williams
CANOEING

 **Pelham Books**

First published in Great Britain by
PELHAM BOOKS LTD
52 Bedford Square
London WC1B 3EF
1977

ISBN 0 7207 0983 0

Filmset and printed in Great Britain by
BAS Printers Limited, Wallop, Hampshire

Contents

Preface 6
1 Equipment
The Kayak 7
  Dimensions 7
  Construction 8
  Selecting a kayak 9
Paddles 14
Crash Helmets 16
Life Preservers 16
Clothing 18
2 Kayak Techniques
Carrying a Canoe 20
Getting in 20
  From a low bank 21
  From shallow water 23
Getting Out 24
  On to a low bank 24
  Into shallow water 24
Setting Off and Landing 25
Basic Strokes 25
  Paddling 25
  Back-paddling 27
  Turning 27
  Moving sideways 30
  Supporting 31
Advanced Strokes 33
  Turning 33
  Moving sideways 36
3 Double-Kayak Techniques
Getting in 37
Setting off 37
Landing 38
Paddling 38
Turning 38
Moving sideways 40
4 Safety and Rescue Techniques
Safety Rules for Canoeists 43
Capsize Drill 45

Rescue Techniques 48
  Swimmer rescue 48
  Eskimo rescue 49
  X rescue method 49
  Double-kayak X rescue 53
The Eskimo Roll 53
Safety on Open Waters 55
Individual Proficiency 58
5 River Canoeing
Reading the Water 59
  Rocks and channels 59
  Rapids 61
Technique 62
  Inspecting rapids 63
  Avoiding obstructions 63
  Turning 65
  Support strokes 65
  Entering fast water 65
  Running aground and portaging 66
6 Planning a River Expedition
Basic Planning 69
Leader's Responsibility 70
  Pre-expedition checks 71
  River briefing 71
Canoe Camping 72
  General items 73
  Packing and loading 73
  Selecting a camp site 79
  Camp fires 80
  Shelters 82
  Camp organization 82
Enjoyment 83
Appendices:
A International System of Grading
   Rivers 84
B British Canoe Union
   Proficiency Tests 85
C National Canoe Federations 87

Preface

Canoeing has become a very popular activity both as a recreational pursuit and as a sport. Its advantages are that it is comparatively cheap to take up, the techniques are not difficult to learn and it has no real age barrier, for canoeing can be enjoyed by the young and those who have long since passed the age for competitive games. Canoeing can be relaxing or exciting depending on whether you wish to paddle sheltered lakes on a summer's day and rest in the sun, or accept the challenge of running your small craft down rapids. It therefore has an appeal for many people ranging from those at school who would like to participate in adventurous training projects, to those who wish to take to the water on their holidays and perhaps fish in a quiet backwater.

Canoeing aims to illustrate the skills, technique and enjoyment of canoeing inland waterways and mountain rivers using the kayak. It is written for the beginner and those canoeists who would like to improve their ability and their knowledge. However, students, teachers and potential instructors/leaders who want to know more about correct technique, canoe safety, and organizing expeditions should also find this compact book informative and interesting.

The author wishes to acknowledge the great assistance given by Gordon Ashman AIIP who took the photographs; also Oliver Cock, Director of Coaching, the British Canoe Union, for his arrangements to reproduce BCU safety rules and proficiency tests. His appreciation is also registered of the kindness of Tyne Canoes Ltd, Twickenham who loaned equipment, and lastly he wishes to acknowledge the help of his son and daughter Christopher and Stephanie who feature in the book.

CHAPTER ONE

Equipment

The object of this chapter is to give guidance and advice as to the most suitable canoeing equipment for river canoeing and inland expeditions using a kayak.

The Kayak
Dimensions
The modern kayak is a form of canoe that has been developed from the Eskimo or Greenland kayak (see Fig. 1). It is fully decked fore and aft, is normally fitted with an individual cockpit(s) and is paddled with a two-bladed paddle. There are various types of kayak on the market, such as the long, specialist single-seat sea designs of about 18 ft (549 cm), competition surf kayaks of 9 ft 8 in (294 cm), slalom competition canoes of about 13 ft 2 in (401 cm) and very compact training canoes of only 7 ft 2 in (219 cm) suitable for baths training.

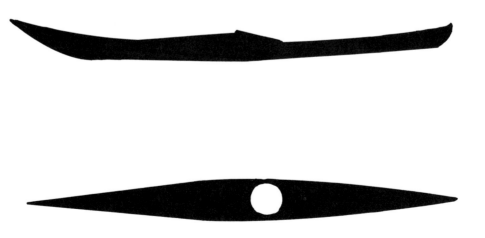

Fig. 1 The forerunner of the modern kayak, the Greenland or Eskimo kayak. Approximate length: 18 ft (549 cm); width: 19 in (48 cm).

Canoeing

As the aim of this book is to consider the techniques and skills that are particularly applicable to river and inland canoeing, attention is therefore concentrated on the types of craft which are most suitable for paddling along waterways and down rapids, and these are shown in Fig. 2.

The dimensions of a canoe are important. A very short canoe of 11 ft (335 cm), though very manoeuvreable, is difficult to steer straight and has little room for the storage of kit. The minimum length for a single-seat canoe for general river work should be about 13 ft $1\frac{1}{2}$ in (400 cm) with a beam of 24 in (61 cm) which conforms to the dimensions of the slalom competition kayak. A very long single-seat kayak of about 16 ft (485 cm), though easy to keep running straight, is not manoeuvreable and this limitation can give problems when negotiating the difficult rock fields which are often found on mountain rivers. Specialist touring kayaks of about 14 ft 6 in (442 cm) with a beam of 24 in (61 cm) are particularly suitable for river expeditions as they possess good maneouvreability and also have adequate internal hull space for storing camping gear. It should be noted that conditions on lakes can at times resemble those found at sea and specialist sea designs are therefore ideal for more exposed, large inland waters.

The touring double-seat kayak must have the capacity to carry two adults plus their camping gear and be able to ride the water well when fully loaded. Because of its greater size it cannot be manœuvred as quickly as a single-seat slalom canoe or single-seat tourer, but a length of about 16 ft (487 cm) and beam around $30\frac{3}{4}$ in (79 cm) will house all the gear you will need for an expedition of several days and, in the hands of a well-trained experienced crew, run grade II and III rapids (see Appendix A) without difficulty.

Construction
The cheapest form of construction is the lath and canvas design comprising marine ply frames, longitudinal wood stringers which are covered with canvas that is proofed with flat or, better still, rubberized paint. This type of canoe is not difficult to build and plans can be purchased with detailed step-by-step instructions, or the canoe can be purchased in kit form. A development of the lath and canvas canoe is the folding single or double canoe which is designed to collapse into easily manageable rucksacks for transportation and storage. The design is costly to make for it requires top-grade materials plus skilled labour. It is normally constructed with mountain ash stringers which, having a straight grain, possess resilience to inpact; the cross frames, stern and bow pieces are made of Finnish birch and the hull and deck are covered with cotton duck canvas coated with several layers of rubberized paint. A well-made lath and canvas canoe, of either the rigid or folding type, will give much pleasure on sheltered inland waterways but if used on more rapid rivers can be easily holed on sharp stones when in shallows, or on rocks — the result being that you may spend almost as much time on repairs as you do on paddling.

A stronger form of construction, now rarely seen, is the type of canoe made from plywood sheets nailed and glued to wood cross-frames. However, this type of hull is difficult to repair and not easy to construct. By far the most popular is the glass-fibre canoe, carefully designed to give the optimum weight/strength ratio. Glass fibre requires no maintenance and will not deteriorate with age. It has a very smooth surface and therefore water friction is reduced to a minimum which makes for a fast craft. It has considerable strength and will not normally break if the craft runs aground or glances off a rock. Should there be damage from a direct impact, the hull can be repaired without leaving a weak spot or area.

A carbon-fibre-enriched kayak consists of a conventionally built glass-fibre light canoe with bunches of carbon fibre placed strategically in the hull so that, despite the lightness of the hull, it has incredible strength and rigidity. This form of construction has been introduced in some slalom canoes but as yet has not been applied to touring designs. The glass-fibre canoe is therefore a viable purchase for river canoeing.

Selecting a kayak
When selecting a glass-fibre kayak for touring, the following points, in addition to those on dimensions already noted, should be considered. Glass-fibre canoes are made in different weights. The slalom canoeist prefers a very light craft and his kayak may weigh as little as 24 lb (11 kg). Although this kayak will have considerable strength, heavier canoes are normally more durable and it is often possible to purchase the same canoe as a standard or extra-reinforced model, weighing about 30 lb (14 kg) and 36 lb (16 kg) respectively. However, take note that you may have to carry your canoe some distance either to and

from a landing area or around weirs and difficult rapids, so the weight of the craft can be important. A slalom or touring-type kayak weighing around 36 lb (16 kg) should give many years of enjoyable paddling and can be easily carried by the average-sized adult. Double kayaks, because of their longer length and the requirement to carry two people, are made of a heavier glass-fibre weave and a 16 ft (487 cm) design will weigh about 60 lb (27 kg). Avoid very heavy designs for they can be very tiring to handle out of water. Well-designed glass-fibre touring kayaks have the following features:

(a) A strong, well-finished hull and decking. The decking of a canoe, though not requiring the same strength and thickness of construction as the hull, should be strong enough to withstand water pressure in the event of a capsize in turbulent water and also to support the weight of a canoe when engaged in X rescue procedure (see Plates 35 and 37).

(b) Built-in or inflatable buoyancy. Built-in buoyancy normally comprises blocks of polyurethane foam built into the bow and stern sections of the canoe and this is sufficient to keep the craft afloat even if filled completely with water. Inflatable buoyancy bags will serve the same purpose but should be firmly attached to the canoe, for if they float out the craft could sink. Ideally, a single seat kayak that is to be used on inland waters should have 30 lb (13 kg) buoyancy at each end. Take note that large inflatable bags can limit the space available for the stowage of kit.

(c) A well-finished cockpit coaming with no sharp edges that could catch knees or thighs.

(d) Rot-proof handling lines at the bow and stern, fitted with 3 in × ¾ in (75 mm × 18 mm) toggles at each end, or a tightly tied rot-proof painter that runs through the deck anchorages so that the cockpit is kept free. Handling lines or painters should be capable of taking a static load of 500 lb (225 kg). In the event of a capsize the handling lines or painter act as a means of contact with the canoe. They also serve as a means of contact when performing the X rescue which necessitates the lifting and emptying of an upturned canoe (see page 49).

(e) A well-designed and well-made spray cover. The spray cover serves to keep water out of the cockpit. It will also help to keep the canoeist warm in bad weather conditions, for when fitted, the lower half of the canoeists' body is fully protected from wind and rain. The cover should fit snugly over the cockpit coaming and is kept in place by the elasticated edge of the cover. A webbing, quick-release strap, sewn across the front of the cover, will ensure that the spray cover is easily released when pulled in any direction.

(f) A comfortable seat. Obviously, this is an important consideration. A well-fitting bucket seat with a padded back rest is often preferred by touring canoeists.

(g) Footrests. These must be easily adjustable and should be of the bar or non-swivelling platform type. If they are the bar type they must be fail safe, that is, in the event of a mishap such as the canoe hitting a rock and the foot being forced past the bar, the bar must break loose to allow the foot to escape.

The British Standards Institution has prepared a standard for the manufacture of British-made canoes. Prospective canoe buyers in Great Britain are advised to look for the BSI Kite Mark on the items they are considering or for the badge of the British Canoe Manufacturers' Association.

Fig. 2 **Types of touring/expedition kayaks**
(not to scale)
SINGLE-SEAT KAYAKS

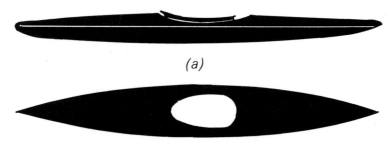

(a)

(a) **White-water tourer**
Approx length: 13 ft 8 ins. (416 cm)
Approx. beam: 24 in (61 cm)
Features: the rockered keel gives manoeuvreability in rough water; it has ample freeboard to shed water and also adequate stowage space for camping gear.

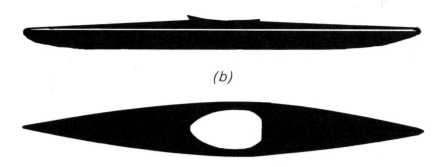

(b)

(b) **Touring kayak**
Approx length: 14 ft 6 in (442 cm)
Approx beam: 24 in (61 cm)
*Features: the long straight keel makes for directional stability and the width and length
provide adequate space for camping gear.*

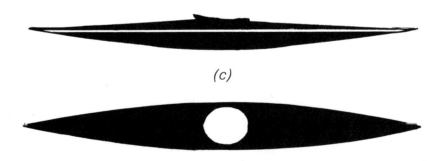

(c)

(c) **Slalom kayak**
Approx length: 13 ft 2 in (401 cm)
Approx beam: 23¾ in (60.5 cm)
*Features: the rockered keel gives great manoeuvreability but the lack of length reduces
directional stability and can make it difficult to steer straight, particularly so for
novices. The low profile enables the kayak to clear slalom gates but stowage space is
not so great as in designs a, b, and d. This kayak is more suited to short-distance
touring than long expeditions.*

11

Canoeing

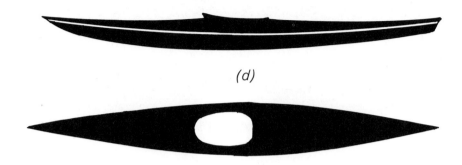

(d)

*(d) **Sea/lake touring kayak***
Approx length: 16 ft (487 cm)
Approx beam: 25 in (63.5 cm)
Features: Ideal for canoeing on lakes as it has ample free-board to shed water,
adequate length to give directional stability and space for camping gear.
(The design is suitable for inshore sea work.)

TWO-SEAT KAYAKS

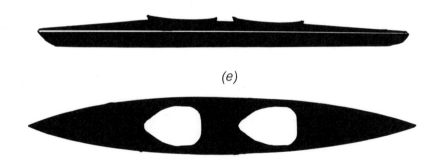

(e)

*(e) **Touring double-seat kayak***
Approx length: 15 ft 11 in (483 cm)
Approx beam: 30¾ in (79 cm)
Features: This kayak will take two crew men and camping gear. The individual
cockpits with well-fitting spray covers and the ample free-board make for a design
suitable to run grade II and III rapids.

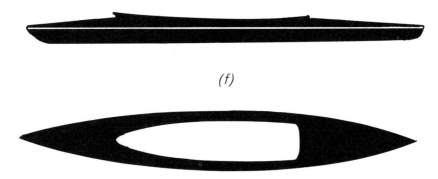

(f)

(f) ***Two-seat kayak*** *(open cockpit)*
Approx length: 15 ft 11 in (483 cm)
Approx beam: 30¾ in (79 cm)
Features: The open cockpit allows an occasional third passenger.

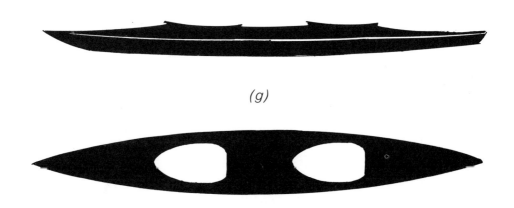

(g)

(g) ***Sea/lake touring kayak***
Approx length: 19 ft (570 cm)
Approx beam: 2 ft 5 in (72.70 cm)
*Features: Ideal for lake canoeing as it has ample free-board to shed water and a high
bow, an Eskimo feature, which gives lift in open water. The kayak's length gives
directional stability and there is ample room for the stowage of camping kit.
(The design is suitable for inshore sea work.)*

13

Canoeing

Paddles

A canoe paddle should be the correct length. The easiest way of checking that the size is right is to stand alongside the paddle and raise your arm so that the fingers just curl over the paddle tip (see Plate 1). To give an idea of the actual size needed, the average man, say, 5 ft 10 in (178 cm) tall, requires a 7 ft 2 in (218 cm) paddle.

Plate 1 Checking the paddle for length; the fingers should just curl over the paddle tip.

There are various forms of paddle on the market, starting with the cheaper novice type which has an alloy shaft (loom) normally covered by plastic sheathing with varnished flat plywood blades fitted at either end. Other paddles are made up of laminated spruce or ash, have curved blades and are much more expensive. Some wooden loom paddles are made in two halves and have curved plywood blades. Brass telescopic ferrules, located at the end of each half, allow the paddle halves to fit together, and locating screws and slots on the ferrules permit adjustments of the alignment of the blades in order to get the correct feathering angle (see page 26). Other paddles on the market comprise wooden looms with curved or flat fibre-glass blades. These paddles may be manufactured all in one or with a centre union as described above. Many touring paddles are fitted with rubber drip rings which serve to stop water running down the loom onto your hands. (See Figs. 3 and 4.)

Flat-bladed paddles are ideal for the novice and as there is no curve in the blade these paddles can be used by canoeists who are right or left dominant. The type of curved paddle that has a centre union can be easily adjusted to suit a left or right dominant paddler. However, should you consider purchasing a paddle that is made in one piece and cannot be adjusted, it is imperative that you have had some experience of paddling before you select the paddle. If you are left dominant (see page 26 and Plate 7) it is essential that when the left blade is pulling through the water the blades are aligned so that the right spoon is uppermost.

Should you buy a paddle that has the right spoon facing downward, it has been made for a right dominant person and you will have the utmost difficulty in paddling.

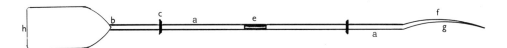

Fig. 3 Parts of the paddle: (a) loom; (b) neck; (c) drip ring; (e) ferrule; (f) back of blade; (g) spoon or front of blade; (h) tip.

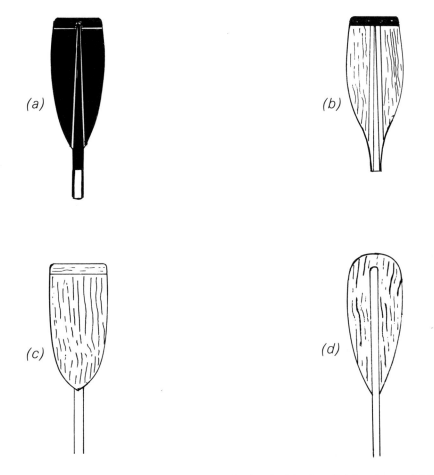

Fig. 4 Some types of blades: (a) flat or curved plastic blade; (b) laminated Mitchwood flat blade; (c) curved plywood touring blade; (d) flat ply general-purpose blade.

Canoeing

Crash Helmets

No canoeist should consider canoeing difficult, rough-water mountain rivers without a crash helmet, for rapids often occur where the river is comparatively shallow, fast and rock strewn, and submerged rocks may not be far under the surface. A capsize in such conditions can give rise to the chance of an underwater collision with a rock, although this is not a common occurrence due to the cushioning effect of water around rocks. When touring rapid rivers it is advisable to wear a crash helmet, particularly where difficult rapids occur. However, when practising basic skills and techniques in calm, well-known water or paddling easy rivers, a crash helmet can be an unnecessary encumbrance. When purchasing a crash helmet look for the type which gives all-round protection, covers the back of the head fully and also gives ear and temple protection. The helmet should be designed to allow water to escape easily and have an easily adjustable chin strap fitted with a chin guard (Fig. 5).

Fig. 5 A crash helmet. The best type is that which gives all-round protection, covering the temples, ears and back of the head. Note the adjustable chin strap fitted with a chin guard.

Life Preservers

I would always advise a canoeist to wear a life preserver no matter how strong a swimmer he is, for water is a powerful force. In normal circumstances a capsize should not cause any undue concern to a person properly trained. However, if a canoeist is not wearing a life preserver and is swept by strong currents down a rapid or away from the shore, he could be in a serious predicament and his life might be at risk.

The type of life preserver which should be worn is often the subject of considerable discussion and depends on many factors, such as the expected use, the degree of difficulty of the water to be paddled, swimming ability of the wearer and whether he is a novice canoeist or not. There are four main types of life preserver that can be considered:

(a) *The buoyancy aid.* In its simplest form this comprises two air pillows which are attached to a webbing or similar harness and worn on the chest and back. They are inflated independently and because of their size have limited buoyancy. They are therefore only suitable for use on river projects and to be worn by good swimmers. They are cheap to buy and offer little restriction to paddling movements.

(b) *The buoyancy-aid waistcoat.* This can be put on like a normal waistcoat and fastened at the front or side. The buoyancy-aid waistcoat has built-in buoyancy which may comprise foam filling giving about $13\frac{1}{2}$ lb (6 kg) of buoyancy; however, there are various types available and it is best to check the manufacturer's specification. The waistcoat-type will give insulation to the body and keep you snug when paddling in cold conditions. In the event of a capsize and immersion of the body in cold water the waistcoat will help to retain the heat of the body which is a significant aspect of its life-preserving properties. Check that zips are strong and if popper studs are fitted they must be tight enough to withstand pressure on the fastening points. Lace-up fittings are also made and these will fasten the jacket securely, but care needs to be taken that the lace is not lost when the buoyancy-aid waistcoat is stored. (See Plates 6 and 11.)

(c) *The two-stage life-jacket.* This life-jacket (Plate 28) has built-in residual buoyancy but can also be inflated. It is normally fairly bulky but uncomplicated,

comprising a neoprene nylon bag covering closed-cell foam which cannot absorb water even if the outer skin is punctured. The jacket is donned over the head and worn on the chest. It is held in position by a webbing strap that runs through a backstrap loop attached to the neck and then the strap is fastened around the waist (Figs. 6 and 7). In the event of a capsize the jacket can be fully inflated by blowing into an air valve which is located in an easily accessible position on the right of the jacket. Full inflation ensures that the body is kept with the chest floating uppermost so that the neck is supported and the face is clear of the water even if the wearer is unconscious.

Two life-jackets of this type which are

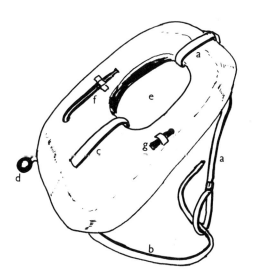

Fig. 6 The two-stage life-jacket (front view): (a) back strap; (b) waist strap; (c) lifting becket; (d) nylon ring; (e) head hole; (f) inflation tube; (g) whistle.

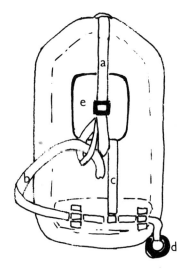

Fig. 7 The two-stage life-jacket (back view): (a) back strap; (b) waist strap; (c) lifting becket; (d) nylon ring; (e) head hole.

Canoeing

made to British Standards Institution specifications are recommended by the British Canoe Union (BCU) as being suitable for canoeing. They are the Ottersport BSI 3595 life-jacket and the Vacum Reflex Life Master, Type 9 life-jacket. These life-jackets have an inherent buoyancy of not less than $13\frac{1}{2}$ lb (6 kg), are compact enough not to impede paddling and have provision for inflation by mouth to full buoyancy of 40 lb (18·16 kg).

(d) *The inflatable, gas-bottle life-jacket.* A compact and light jacket based on the aircrew 'Mae West'; it can be inflated in the event of a capsize by the release of a CO_2 valve. It is more expensive than the other life preservers listed and after each inflation requires a new CO_2 bottle. The jacket is built with the majority of its buoyancy in the front so as to float the body face-uppermost with the neck completely supported.

Before finally deciding on a specific jacket take note that the British Canoe Union state that not all life-jackets are suitable for canoeing even though they conform to BSI 3595. The Safety Committee of the BCU recommend the two jackets noted in (c) above, which should be worn by beginners.

Clothing

The type of clothing worn for canoeing should vary according to the time of year and the anticipated weather conditions. Clothing must be both practical and comfortable and never so tight that it restricts paddling. Outlined in the following paragraphs are items of clothing suitable for summer conditions, adverse weather and, for those experienced canoeists who wish to canoe all the year round, cold conditions.

A long-sleeve or quarter-sleeve light cotton shirt is comfortable for summer cruises and will give protection from sunburn, an important factor as the sun's reflection off the water can be extreme. Nylon shorts are light and dry quickly. Old gym shoes or basketball boots (with holes cut in the sides to let water out before you board after wading) will protect the feet. It is best to wear wool socks as well for they prevent chafing and, even when wet, will keep the feet warm. A light canvas cap with a neck flap will protect the head and a green-lined peak helps to reduce the glare from the water.

Adverse weather demands clothing with greater insulating properties. One or two rugby-type loose-fitting jerseys, or a wool sweater over a light wool shirt, can help protect the upper body. Over this can be worn an anorak fitted with elasticated cuffs to stop water seeping up the wrists, a hood with a draw string and a large zip map pocket located on the front. Track-suit or sweat-suit pants of soft warm wool should keep the lower half snug. Wool mitts will protect the hands yet allow a firm grip on the paddle. A soft wool cap that can be pulled well down over the ears will protect the head.

If you should canoe under cold conditions the selection of clothing to be worn needs great care. If inadequate clothing is worn and the body becomes soaked, perhaps through running heavy waves or rapids, the risk of exposure is considerable. In the event of a capsize and a bail-out the consequences could be very serious. The bottom half of the body can be best protected by wet-suit trousers with wet-suit boots. The upper half can be protected by a neoprene rubber jacket with a cotton shirt worn underneath to prevent chafing. Silk gloves covered by neoprene rubber gloves will keep the fingers and hands warm but should not be so tight fitting that they restrict hand movements. A light woollen scarf around the neck will help seal any heat loss from around that area and, if required, can be pulled up to cover the lower half of the face. In addition, the head needs to be protected. Remember that heat lost is energy lost, and a fair paddle can require considerable energy. Quite low water-temperatures can often be present in the height of summer, particularly in glacier-fed rivers or lakes. Mountain rivers, lakes and the sea can also have low temperatures at this time of year. The selection of the right clothing is therefore important to the comfort, enjoyment and safety of the canoeist.

CHAPTER TWO

Kayak Techniques

This chapter outlines the techniques and skills required to handle and manoeuvre a kayak.

Carrying a Canoe

The average single-seat kayak can be quite easily carried on the shoulder. Assuming you are standing alongside the craft on the left side facing the cockpit, place the paddle inside the canoe, grip the underside of the far coaming at the point of balance and lift the canoe with both hands on to your right shoulder. Move the left hand forward to hold the apex of the coaming to steady the canoe. If the canoe has to be carried some distance and you are wearing a life-jacket, lower the coaming to rest on the jacket in order to ease the load.

When two people carry a canoe, one person takes the bow and the other the stern on the opposite side. The double canoe is best carried by two people and on the shoulder if there is some distance to be covered; otherwise it can be carried over comparatively short distances with arms hooked around the bow and stern.

Getting In

Boarding a canoe requires a variation of

Plate 2 Check the canoe and equipment before setting off.

technique dependent on the size of the canoe cockpit and whether you are getting in from a bank or from shallow water. The touring canoe normally has a fairly large cockpit opening and is easy to board; the slalom and white water designs have a more compact, smaller cockpit and are a little more difficult to get into. The following techniques describe how to get into a canoe to the right:

From a low bank
Method 1 (slalom-type cockpit)
(a) Draw the kayak, which is facing upstream, close to the bank and place the paddle across the deck just behind the cockpit with the other blade flat on the bank.
(b) Crouch beside the cockpit and grasp the shaft and also the inside of the rim of the cockpit with the right hand. Sit on the shaft with the left hand placed palm-down across the paddle shaft close to the left blade.
(c) Move your feet into the canoe. (Plate 3.)
(d) Lean back to take the weight on the hands, then slide into the cockpit.
(e) Sit up, move the paddle in front of you, then secure the spray cover.

Plate 3 Getting in from a low bank – see Method 1

Canoeing

Method 2 (touring cockpit)
(a) Check that your paddle is alongside the canoe, and that the canoe is close to the bank and facing upstream.
(b) Kneel down and hold the bank with your left hand in line with the apex of the cockpit and grasp the apex with your right.
(c) Place the right foot into the cockpit as far forward as it will go and transfer your weight to that foot.

(d) Place your left foot behind the right in the middle of the canoe and quickly sit down, at the same time releasing your left hand from the bank but grasping the paddle.
(e) Rest the paddle across your lap and, if necessary, adjust your position in the boat by placing your hands behind you on the gunwales so that you are comfortable before you set off. Secure the spray cover.

Plate 4 Getting in from a low bank — see Method 3.

Method 3 (touring cockpit)
(a) Check that the canoe is close to the bank and facing upstream.
(b) Lay the paddle to rest with one blade flat on the bank at right angles to the canoe so that the loom crosses the apex of the cockpit. (Plate 4.)
(c) Crouch on the bank and grasp the paddle and apex of the cockpit with the right hand; take hold of the loom near the blade on the bank with the left hand.
(d) The paddle acts as a stabilizer for it supports the weight of the body as you reach out to enter the canoe and holds the canoe secure. The movements of the feet are the same as in Method 2.

From shallow water
Method 4 (touring and slalom cockpits)
(a) This method can be used in water shin to thigh deep. Firstly, stand facing the bows, which should point upstream, and alongside the seat of the canoe, with the paddle in the right hand.
(b) Grasp the far gunwale just behind the seat with your right hand, which should also hold the paddle, and place your right foot well forward into the centre of the canoe. As you do so, grasp the left gunwale just behind the seat with your left hand. (Plate 5.)

Plate 5 Getting in from shallow water – see Method 4.

Canoeing

(c) Bend your left knee to lower your body almost into the seat. Take the weight with the hands on the gunwales behind you. (If you are boarding a slalom-type canoe it will be necessary to lower the body to sit on the back of the rim of the cockpit then slide down into the seat. This requires practice as the body has to be balanced. If difficulty is experienced, the paddle can be held with both hands across the back of the cockpit rim to lie flat on the water and at right angles to the canoe so as to act as an outrigger and partially support the body.)

(d) Lower yourself into the cockpit allowing the left foot to be drawn into the canoe once water has drained from the shoe.

(e) Adjust your position in the cockpit. Fix the spray cover.

Getting Out

The following techniques describe how to get out to the left.

On to a low bank
Method 1 (slalom-type cockpit)
(a) Manœuvre the canoe so that it faces upstream alongside the bank. Release the spray cover.
(b) Place the paddle across the deck just behind the cockpit with the left blade flat on the bank.
(c) Grasp the shaft and the rim of the cockpit with the right hand and the shaft just outboard of the canoe with the left hand.
(d) Placing the weight of your body on the paddle, slide out of the cockpit to sit on the paddle shaft and cockpit rim.
(e) Place the left foot onto the bank then

carefully move across to the bank. Retain a hold on the canoe.

Method 2 (touring cockpit)
(a) Manœuvre the canoe so that it faces upstream alongside the bank. Release the spray cover and place your paddle on the bank or across the cockpit. Hold the bank with your left hand.
(b) Reach forward with your right hand to grasp the apex of the cockpit coaming. Bring the right foot behind the left as far back in the cockpit as they will come and directly in the middle of the canoe.
(c) Pull yourself forward with the right hand so that your weight is directly over the centre of the canoe and then place your left foot on the bank.
(d) Transfer your weight to this foot and remove the right foot from the canoe to the bank, but retain your hold on the canoe.

Into shallow water
Method 3 (touring and slalom-type cockpits)
(a) Undo the spray cover. Place your paddle in your right hand and put both hands behind to grasp the gunwales in line with the seat on either side.
(b) Bring your feet as far back as they will come and then raise yourself from the seat by taking your weight on your heels and hands. (When disembarking from a slalom-type canoe it will be necessary to raise the body to sit on the rear rim of the cockpit. The paddle may be used to lie flat on the water held with both hands across the back of the cockpit rim at right angles to the canoe so as to act as an outrigger and partially support the body.)

(c) Slide your left hand further aft and raise your left foot over the side and place it on the river bed.

(d) Place your right foot over the left side to the river bed, at the same time quickly releasing the left hand from the gunwale and moving the right hand from the right gunwale to the coaming to retain the canoe.

Setting Off and Landing

When setting off or landing where there is a current, use the current to assist you. Set off upstream into the current so that the water will help move the craft out and clear of the bank before turning to paddle downstream. You will find that setting off this way gives greater control of the craft and there is no risk of the canoe being swept along the side of the bank fouling branches overhanging the water or running into shallows. Similarly, when landing turn the canoe to face the current, select a suitable landing spot, then paddle forward to manœuvre the canoe to where you wish to disembark.

Basic Strokes

Basic strokes are those strokes which achieve a desired manœuvre in the simplest way. They are as follows:

Paddling

Hold the paddle just wider than shoulder width (see Plate 6) and sit relaxed and comfortable in the canoe with your feet against the footrest or frame of the canoe and knees against the

Plate 6 Hold the paddle just wider than shoulder width, then get the feel of the paddle before you board. The canoeist is wearing a Harishok buoyancy-aid waistcoat.

sides or knee bars if fitted. Paddling with a 'feathered paddle' or blades set at an angle to one another allows the canoeist to exercise leverage on the paddle with comparatively little effort. One hand permits the loom of the paddle to rotate while the other lightly grips the other half of the shaft. If the left hand acts as the gripping hand and the right allows the loom to rotate, the paddles are set so that when the left blade is in the water pulling, the right blade is at 90° to the left paddle blade with the spoon uppermost. If the right hand acts as the gripping hand, the left paddle blade is also set at 90° to the right but the right spoon surface faces downward when the left paddle is in the water. Paddling requires effort from both arms and the push forward on the loom from the upper arm is as important as the pull on the paddle in the water. To achieve this

important push, the wrist of the raised arm is always extended to a position necessary for force to be laid on the paddle. A simple explanation may be obtained from considering the position of the arm and wrist when a garden roller is pushed. The wrist is extended in order to get maximum leverage and never kept in the same plane as the forearm. Assuming you are now ready to paddle, check that the paddle blades are at 90° to one another with the spoon blades facing the right way, this will depend on which is the controlling or gripping hand. With the trunk inclined slightly forward, reach as far forward as you can with the right arm straight and place the right paddle blade in the water close to the canoe and vertical. The blade should be covered to the neck and the left arm bent (see Plate 7). Pull with the right arm and simultaneously push with the left arm

Plate 7 Paddling: note the extended position of the left wrist so as to give power when the left arm pushes forward.

Plate 8 Paddling: the upper arm is fully extended, the lower arm pulls right through.

which moves forward with the wrist extended. The left arm is fully straightened so as to exercise maximum leverage (the upper hand should not be allowed to travel higher than the level of the eyes). Repeat the stroke on the other side. Make long relaxed strokes with the paddle pivoting rhythmically around an imaginary point in front of your chest (see Plate 8).

Back-paddling
Back-paddling is used to stop the canoe, to move backwards, or hold the canoe against a current without drifting downstream as in the ferry glide (page 63). Use the back of the blades and paddle backwards placing the blades vertically and as far back as possible without discomfort. Lean back and make strong rhythmical strokes with a full

extension of the lower arm.

Turning
To change direction, simply paddle harder on the opposite side to which the turn is to be made but, at the same time, not breaking the paddle rhythm. A quicker turn can be made by making a back-paddle stroke on the side to which you want to turn. Other basic steering and turning strokes are:

Stern rudder. The stern rudder is a simple stroke made to steer a single or double canoe that is underway. It is of particular use when coming alongside. Hold the paddle with the hands in the normal paddling position on the loom and lower the paddle towards the stern post on the side to which the turn is desired. The spoon of the blade faces the hull. Reach back to extend the rear-most arm and

27

Plate 9 The stern rudder.

place the paddle in the water near the stern (see Plate 9). To increase the angle of turn push the paddle away; to reduce the angle bring in the paddle to the stern. *Sweep and reverse sweep.* To turn a canoe around, make a sweep stroke from the bow on one side in the following way and a reverse sweep from the stern on the other side. To make a sweep stroke hold the paddle as for normal paddling and reach as far forward as you can. Place the blade vertical, and with the spoon facing away from the hull, into the water near the bow on the opposite side to which the turn is intended (see Plate 10). Sweep the paddle out and away from the canoe around to the stern through 180° (see Plate 11). The outboard arm should be extended and

the inboard arm kept low. As the canoeist becomes more expert the angle of the blade can be changed slightly so that the upper edge is angled away from the hull. As the sweep is made, the canoeist can now lean slightly on the paddle and then, with practice, more heavily. The stroke has now developed into a partial scull which gives support (see sculling, page 32). The reverse sweep is the same as the sweep except that it is carried out in reverse, i.e. from the stern to the bows, and commences with the spoon of the blade facing inwards to the stern (see Plate 12 and 13). The same blade angle as for the sweep stroke can be applied later to give greater effect and also support. (See page 39 for double-canoe techniques.)

Plate 10 The start of the sweep stroke.

*Plate 11 The finish of the sweep stroke
and the canoe has turned almost 90°.
The canoeist is wearing a Bailey
buoyancy-aid waistcoat.*

*Plate 12 The start of the reverse sweep
stroke.*

*Plate 13 The finish of the reverse sweep
stroke.*

Canoeing

Moving sideways
Draw stroke. The draw stroke is made to move the canoe sideways and can be used to draw into or away from the bank and to miss obstructions. Raise the paddle up with the blade parallel to the canoe and the spoon facing the hull, then place the blade into the water opposite the seat about 3 ft (90 cm) from the canoe. The upper hand is about level with the mouth. The paddle is now drawn almost to the side of the canoe by the lower arm pulling and the upper arm pushing (see Plate 14). The movement is continued at right angles towards the stern with the edge of the blade leading to form an 'L', then knifed out of the water and repeated. If the stroke is made towards the bow or stern it will draw that end. With practice the paddle can be lifted high and leaned onto so that greater leverage is obtained and a more powerful stroke made (see Plate 23).
Sculling draw stroke. The sculling draw stroke can be used to draw a canoe sideways and also to draw it diagonally forwards or backwards. It is a useful stroke to apply when manœuvring into or out of an awkward landing place. Raise the paddle to the side and dip one blade into the water, with the spoon facing the canoe, about 1 ft (30 cm) from the seat parallel with the hull. Do not completely immerse the paddle at first (so that you can see what you are doing) but the loom should be as vertical as possible. Move the paddle continuously backwards and forwards parallel to the canoe. The leading edge is turned slightly outwards as each sweep is made, by twisting the lower wrist so that water pressure builds up under the spoon of the blade. Once the effect of the stroke is

Plate 14 *The draw stroke. Push with the upper arm and pull with the lower so as to draw the blade almost to the side of the canoe (see text).*

felt the sweep may be made slower, the paddle immersed deeper so that the lower hand is just above the surface and a slight pull is exercised on the loom in each sweep (see Plate 15). Now place the paddle diagonally forward or backward from the cockpit to draw the canoe in a diagonal direction. The paddle is swept at right angles to an imaginary line from the cockpit to the position required.

Supporting
The paddle can be used to prevent a capsize by obtaining considerable support from the resistance of the water against the downward pressure of the flat paddle blade.

Slap support. This is a simple form of recovery when on the verge of capsizing. Reach out with the paddle (spoon up) about a foot above the water and at right angles to the hull. The outboard arm is straight, the inboard hand kept low. Now heel the canoe over and then right the canoe by pushing down with the outboard arm. The blade is recovered by turning it through 90° to knife out of the water. Increase the heel of the canoe and repeat the process either side but remembering to keep both hands low. Progress so that you can sit with the paddle held resting on the deck in front, heel the canoe over until the spray cover is awash, reach out and push up (see Plate 16). Practise on both sides.

Plate 15 The sculling draw stroke. Scull the paddle forwards and backwards to catch the water and pull the canoe sideways (see text).

Plate 16 Preventing a capsize with the slap support. The blade is kept flat and the outboard arm straight.

Sculling for support. Sculling for support is a development of slap support. The paddle will give prolonged support if sculled on or just below the surface, so reach out at right angles to the cockpit with the spoon of the paddle facing upward. The outboard arm is straight and the paddle is kept low. Sweep the paddle forward and backward on the surface in a small arc. In the forward movement, the forward edge is raised slightly; in the sweep towards the stern the rear edge is raised. Widen the arc to about 4 ft (120 cm) and make the sweep a continuous movement, then lean on the paddle. The paddle will support you even though the canoe tilts so that the deck is awash (see Plate 17). The low paddle brace and the eskimo roll are developments of this stroke (see pages 65 and 53).

Plate 17 *Preventing a capsize by sculling for support. Note that the sculling action of the paddle near the surface will give continuous support even though the deck is awash.*

Advanced Strokes

Advanced strokes are an extension of basic strokes or a mixture of two or more basic strokes. The following are advanced strokes but take note that the screw roll (page 53) is also included in this category.

Turning

Low telemark. The low telemark is a spectacular and exhilarating form of fast turn (see Plate 18). When paddling down fast water it can be used to turn suddenly and move into a suitable landing place. To perform the turn to the

Plate 18 *The low telemark turn being used to cut out of the current.*

right, paddle forward to get up a fair speed then stretch out with the paddle on the right side towards the stern keeping the paddle low. The right arm is fully extended with the paddle spoon uppermost. Place the paddle on the surface of the water with the leading edge raised slightly. Lean forward, tilt the canoe over by moving your hips and place your weight on the paddle. The water under the paddle will support you initially, due to the pressure formed under the back of the blade caused by the angle of the blade and the speed of the canoe. Once the canoe has turned through 90° and the momentum dies, sweep the paddle with the blade at the same angle in an arc towards the bow (which will draw the bow even further around), then right the craft with a movement of the hips.

High telemark. The high telemark can be used to draw the canoe out of a fast run of water by reaching into an eddy behind a boulder or obstruction. In order to make a high telemark to the right, lift the paddle up so that the left arm is held above the head (see Plates 19 and 20). Reach out to the right towards the stern with the blade spoon downward and almost vertical. The leading edge is raised slightly. Now lean on the paddle. As the canoe turns and the forward momentum dies, sweep the paddle forward to the bow and then sit up. Full use is made of the support under the paddle given by the eddy turning upstream against the blade and the canoe will almost pivot around the position of the paddle. Like the low telemark, the turn is very fast.

Bow rudder. The bow rudder stroke is a

Plate 19 The high telemark. Note how the blade catches the water and the fast turn commences (see also Plate 20).

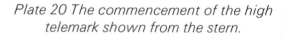

Plate 20 The commencement of the high telemark shown from the stern.

Plate 21 The bow rudder. The stroke is demonstrated with the blade partially exposed to show the spoon, normally fully immersed, facing the hull. Note from the turbulence near the stern how quickly the turn has commenced.

way of turning the canoe from the bow. To make a turn to the right, move the left hand across the face so that it is held above the right shoulder; in doing so the right blade assumes a vertical position, the spoon facing the hull. Lean the trunk forward and place the right blade into the water (see Plate 21). The effectiveness of the turn will depend on how close the paddle is placed to the bow and on the speed of the canoe. After the canoe has turned sufficiently, carry through into a normal paddle stroke without removing the paddle from the water.

Cross bow rudder. This stroke is sometimes known as the Colorado hook and is another way of turning the canoe from the bow. To turn to the right, twist the trunk, moving the whole paddle

Plate 22 The cross bow rudder. The spoon of the blade faces the hull. The turn is fast and exhilarating.

Plate 23 The commencement of the high draw stroke. This is a much more powerful stroke than the draw stroke (see Plate 14). The canoeist will lean heavily onto the paddle.

around to the right, then place the left blade vertically into the water with the spoon facing the hull (see Plate 22). The degree of turn achieved depends on how far the blade is from the bow and on the speed of the canoe. If the turn becomes unstable, lift the left blade and scull the right blade out from near the stern to obtain support and also to continue the turning movement.

Moving sideways
High draw. The high draw stroke is a development of the draw but a much more powerful stroke. The canoeist reaches out with the paddle away from the canoe to place the blade parallel to the canoe with the spoon facing the hull (see Plate 23). As the stroke commences he leans on the paddle, then draws the

paddle towards the hull by pulling with the lower arm and fully extending the upper. The movement is then continued at right angles towards the stern with the edge of the blade leading to form an 'L', then knifed out of the water and the stroke repeated.

Moving draw. The moving draw is a static stroke that will move the canoe sideways to miss an obstruction. The canoe is moving forward and the first position of the high draw is held but with the paddle blade slightly angled away from the bow so that the water pressure under the blade pulls the canoe sideways as it glides on. The paddle can then be partially drawn to the side of the canoe to draw the craft further and turned to pull through as in a normal paddle stroke.

CHAPTER THREE

Double-Kayak Techniques

The techniques required to paddle and manœuvre a double touring canoe are based on the same skills needed to control the single kayak. However, these skills must often be performed simultaneously by the two crewmen and therefore each needs a clear understanding of the other and of individual responsibilities. The bowman acts as look-out and informs the sternman, who is the 'captain' of the craft, of what is ahead — perhaps shoals, rocks or the run of the current. Unless told to do otherwise the bowman just keeps up his paddling stroke. Practice is essential if there is to be a clear understanding between both paddlers with their reactions to situations being automatic and in unison. This understanding can soon be achieved and basic strokes applied with uniformity and precision.

The double touring kayak has certain merits. It provides pleasure for two people at a lower cost than two single kayaks and affords companionship for the paddlers. It is a comparatively faster craft than a single tourer and has ample storage space to take all the gear needed by two people on a camping tour, plus

their food. Generally speaking, it is a comfortable and stable craft.

Getting in
Place the canoe in the water with the bow facing into the current or into the wind, whichever is the stronger. The sternman holds the bow of the canoe against the bank while the bowman boards (see Methods 2 and 3 on pages 22 and 23, also Plates 4 and 49). Once the bowman has fastened his spray cover he holds the canoe close to the bank while the sternman boards. In order to set off in water up to thigh deep use the technique described in Method 4 (Plate 5) to board the craft. The sternman holds the bow of the canoe into the current (or wind) while the bowman boards and fastens his spray cover; then the bowman keeps the canoe into the current (or wind) by paddling gently while the sternman boards.

Setting Off
When setting off on a river, paddle upstream and at a slight angle to the current so that the canoe moves steadily out from the bank under control to clear any obstructions such as branches or

Canoeing

rocks close in. Now turn the craft in deeper water before commencing to paddle down river. If the boarding place is hemmed in by trees or rocks, it may be necessary to draw the canoe out sideways using the draw stroke (see Plates 14 and 28), or draw out diagonally forward or backward with the sculling draw (see Plate 15).

Landing

Turn the canoe to face upstream and select your landing place, then paddle into the current to the landing point. If need be, use the stern rudder stroke to control the final glide alongside. Should the point be difficult to approach it may be necessary to finally draw or scull alongside the bank. Once alongside, the bowman holds the bow into the bank while the sternman disembarks. The sternman now holds the bow while the bowman gets out.

Paddling

A well-trained double-kayak crew will paddle many miles of river in a day without undue fatigue. Practise long relaxed strokes so that the craft glides along with little real effort placed on the paddles (see Plate 24). However, with the aid of the current it is possible to maintain 3 to 5 mph (5 to 8 kph) for many hours.

Turning

The double canoe can be made to change direction by paddling a little harder on the opposite side to which you wish to turn or by leaning slightly to the opposite side of the direction of the intended turn. The stern rudder stroke (see Plate 9) performed by the sternman will turn the canoe on or off course with no great loss of speed if the bowman keeps up his paddle stroke. The following are methods of turning a double canoe right around:

Plate 24 Paddling. Make long relaxed strokes. A well-trained double kayak crew will paddle many miles in a day without undue fatigue.

Plate 25 Turning the canoe around. The commencement of the sweep from the bow and reverse sweep from the stern (also see Plate 26)

Sweep and reverse sweep. The bowman makes a sweep from the bow on the opposite side to which the turn is to be made and the sternman makes a reverse sweep from the stern on the opposite side to that of the bowman's paddle. The strokes are made in unison so that the canoe pivots around a point amidships and the craft turns easily (see Plates 25 and 26).

Plate 26 The finish of the sweep and reverse sweep strokes. Note how the canoe has turned through 90°.

Canoeing

Telemark. Paddle to get up a reasonable speed, then, on a pre-arranged signal, stop paddling and, without any undue haste, both crew members place their paddles to one side of the craft as described for the telemark on page 33 but with both the blades parallel (see Plate 27). The crew now lean on the paddles so that the canoe tilts and the gunwale is awash. The canoe will turn very quickly. As the momentum dies, sweep both paddles forward to the bow and sit up. If necessary, finish off with one sweep stroke with both paddles on the opposite side to ensure that the craft has turned almost 180°.

Moving Sideways

The techniques used to draw a single kayak sideways, namely the draw and the sculling drawstroke, are suitable for use by the double-canoe crew (see Plate 28) but all movements must be synchronized and made in unison to have maximum effect. The moving draw stroke as described on page 36 can also be used to miss a rock and other obstructions when the canoe is underway. The ferry glide, described on page 63, is a method of moving the canoe sideways by utilizing the pressure of the water against the hull to achieve this manœuvre and can be adapted for use by

Plate 27 The telemark will turn the canoe right around. Lean on the paddle until the forward momentum dies, then sweep the paddle toward the bow (see text). Chevron buoyancy-aid waistcoats are worn.

Plate 28 The commencement of the draw stroke. Note the lean onto the paddles in order to make a powerful stroke. Two-stage life-jackets are worn.

Plate 29 Moving diagonally sideways to the right with the bow rudder and reverse sweep strokes (see text).

Canoeing

the double-kayak crew. In a weak current only the sternman may need to back-paddle but a fast current will require both crewmen to back-paddle in unison to hold the craft against the water.

Bow rudder and reverse sweep. The bow rudder and reverse sweep is an advanced technique. The canoe must be under way and travelling faster than the current. A bow rudder stroke is made by the bowman on the side away from the obstruction ahead and simultaneously the sternman makes a quarter sweep out from the stern on the side of the obstruction (see Plate 29). If the blades are placed correctly the canoe will move diagonally away from the obstruction in the direction of the bowman's paddle. If one blade is placed too far out or too close to the hull, one stroke will overcome the effect of the other and the canoe will start to turn slightly and no diagonal movement will be achieved. With practice the sternman can sense any tendency to broach and can correct the canoe's alignment by increasing or decreasing the angle of his paddle out from the stern.

CHAPTER FOUR

Safety and Rescue Techniques

Canoeing is a challenging activity that can incorporate the excitement of running rapids and the enjoyment of touring wild areas and camping in remote and beautiful country. As in all adventurous pursuits there can be an element of risk and therefore it is very important that the possibility of accidents is reduced to a minimum. Safety concerns both the individual canoeist and the group. It encompasses the correct instruction of the individual, selection and proper use of the right equipment, thorough practice at capsize and rescue drill and adherence to safety rules. The following safety code is based on rules produced by the British Canoe Union.

Safety Rules for Canoeists

1. *Don't canoe if you cannot swim.* You must be able to swim 50 yards in light clothing and tread water for at least a minute in the kind of water conditions to be encountered.
2. *Don't go out alone.* Three canoes are a safe minimum. In the event of a mishap assistance will be at hand.
3. *Wear a life jacket.* The British Canoe Union (BCU) advocates that beginners should always wear an approved life-jacket conforming to British Standard 3595 which is a two-stage jacket with inherent buoyancy of not less than 6 kg ($13\frac{1}{2}$ lb) (see page 17). Such a life-jacket should always be worn (irrespective of how good a canoeist or swimmer you are) when a capsize would be dangerous, eg, in the sea at all times or on cold or swollen rivers or open water. It is recommended by the BCU that, subject to the regulations covering the operative authority and at the leader's discretion, experienced canoeists who are good swimmers may dispense with life-jackets on some rivers and inland waterways. This dispensation should only be given if weather, temperature and water conditions are good, and there is no element of danger.
4. *Check your canoe for buoyancy.* Canoes must have built-in buoyancy or buoyancy bags. In the event of a capsize the buoyancy should remain in place and enable the canoe to float level (see page 9).
5. *Ask about local conditions: tides, currents, rapids and weather changes can be dangerous.*
6. *Keep away from weirs as they are*

Canoeing

dangerous. The weir (see Fig. 8) is the most dangerous of river hazards. The almost vertical fall of water from one level to another causes a large stopper wave to form with strong eddies downstream. An unwary canoeist capsizing in the weir could be held by the stopper wave and drowned in the turbulence. Should he manage to break through the wave he may be returned to the turbulent water by the strong eddy.

7. *Don't put more people in a canoe than it is designed to carry.*

8. *Don't wear wellingtons or heavy clothes.* You cannot swim in boots and heavy jackets.

9. *Don't change places.* If you want to change places in the double kayak pull into the bank to do so.

10. *Keep clear of other craft.* If the river is a navigation keep well clear of boats and ships; also keep away from moored barges, particularly those moored in a fast current for an unwary canoeist could be swept against the hull, then capsized and forced under the barge.

11. *Don't right a capsized canoe. Hang on to it. It will float but you may not.* In the event of a capsize leave the canoe upside down and stay with the craft. Swim into shore with the craft as described on page 46. Only in exceptional circumstances should you leave the canoe, eg if the canoe is drifting onto a dangerous hazard such as a sluice or weir.

12. *Don't have slack deck lines, loose ropes or gear in the cockpit; they are dangerous in an emergency.*

13. *Do tell someone where you are going and how long you will be.*

14. *Always check your canoe and equipment for serviceability before you set out.*

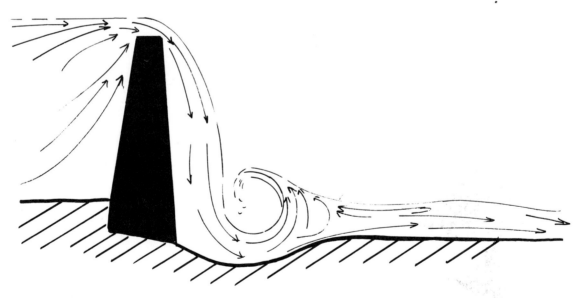

Fig. 8 Keep away from weirs: the large stopper wave can trap a capsized canoeist; the strong eddy just below can draw upstream any canoe that may get too near on the downstream side.

Capsize Drill

Capsize drill is a vital part of a canoeist's basic training. A person who is afraid of capsizing will never make a good canoeist for he will not be able to relax and perfect the skills of the sport, including support strokes which are his safeguard when in turbulent water. Correct capsize technique will ensure that you can easily, and without panic, extract yourself from the close-fitting snug cockpit, then calmly retrieve the paddle and canoe. Practise with an experienced partner in sheltered calm water. When the canoe capsizes allow the craft to turn completely upside down. Let the paddle go and lean as far forward as you can, then release the front of the spray cover with both hands by pulling on the quick-release strap. Now put both hands behind you on the gunwale and roll forward and down out of the cockpit (see Plate 30). You will find that the water assists the movement and, provided you apply the correct technique, it is easier to get out of the

Plate 30 Capsize drill. Demonstrating on the surface the position adopted when the canoe is upside-down and after the spray cover has been released. From this position under the water the canoeist would roll forward and down out of the cockpit.

Plate 31 Capsize drill. Retrieve your paddle, then go to the upstream end and swim to the bank taking care not to break the airlock.

canoe when upside-down than on the surface. Take note that should you lean back and try to push or wriggle your body out of the cockpit, this makes for a much more difficult exit and the inside of the cockpit coaming can take the skin off your thighs and shins. On breaking the surface, retrieve your paddle and leave the craft upside-down so that the airlock is not broken and no more water will enter. If you are on a river and intend to beach the canoe to empty it, swim to the upstream end and take hold of the painter or toggle. Do not rest on the canoe as this may break the airlock and let more water into the hull. Swim on your back towards the bank using the life-saving leg kick (see Plate 31). You will find that though you may be swept downstream, if the canoe is positioned at an angle to the current this will help to ferry-glide you and your craft in to the bank. Capsize drill can be followed by X rescue practice (see page 49) with two or three canoeists taking it in turns to capsize and then be rescued.

Plate 32 Emptying the canoe. Depress one end (see also Plate 33).

Plate 33 After depressing the canoe, quickly lift the end, turn the canoe over and rock the craft so that water pours out. Repeat the process until the canoe is empty.

Canoeing

Rescue Techniques

There are a number of canoe rescue techniques that can be employed when going to the aid of a capsized canoeist. The techniques described below are particularly suited for river canoe projects and require only one rescuer to be effective. They can also be used in emergencies on open water.

Swimmer rescue

In the unlikely event of a canoeist being trapped in the cockpit of his craft after a capsize, a swimmer can right the canoeist in the following way. The rescuer swims over the hull so that his legs hang down on the approach side. He holds onto the canoe hull by locking one arm around the gunwale of the upturned canoe while his free hand reaches down and grasps the forearm of the victim (Fig. 9). The rescuer now grips the victim's arm with both hands near the elbow and pulls the canoeist's arm up and over the canoe hull so as to bend the victim's trunk forward and close to the decking. The rescuer then swings his body back with his knees against the hull so that the canoe and its occupant rotate upward to the surface (Fig. 10). Note that too powerful a pull can dislocate the victim's shoulder or pull him right over into the water on the other side.

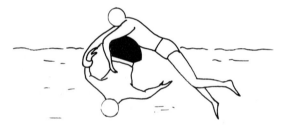

Fig. 9 Swimmer rescue. The rescuer swims across the upturned hull then reaches down and grasps the forearm of the trapped canoeist.

Fig. 10 Swimmer rescue. The rescuer now grasps the victim's forearm with both hands and pulls him forward, then places his knees against the hull, leans back and rotates the canoeist and canoe upright.

Eskimo rescue

The Eskimo rescue or bow grab is a form of rescue whereby a capsized canoeist does not 'bail out' but remains in his craft and signals for help. In some designs of canoe such as the Greenland kayak it is possible to remain in the cockpit and, by dog paddling with the hands, swim with the head above the water. This is also possible in some forms of slalom and touring canoes, particularly if the life-jacket is fully inflated. A canoeist can with practice, remain in his cockpit holding his breath under water and, by leaning forward to raise his hands and banging on the hull of his craft, attract the attention of a nearby fellow paddler. The rescuer then quickly moves to place his bow near the cockpit of the overturned craft and the capsized canoeist grabs the bow and pulls himself into the upright position (see Plate 34). Like all techniques, the Eskimo rescue needs practice, not so much to perfect skill for it is a simple manoeuvre, but to gain confidence.

X rescue method

In the event of a capsize when canoeing a river that has steep muddy banks above deep water, emptying and re-boarding the canoe at the side of the river can be a difficult operation. Similarly if the river is wide, or when on a lake, time can be lost

Plate 34 The Eskimo rescue or bow grab. The capsized canoeist remains in his cockpit, grabs the bow of the rescue craft and pushes himself upright.

swimming to the bank in possibly cold conditions to empty then re-board the craft. The X rescue method saves inconvenience and time and therefore reduces the risk of exposure. This method of rescue enables a single canoeist to empty and right another capsized canoe and then assist the canoeist to re-board his craft. With practice the whole operation can be completed in less than a minute. The rescuer takes charge of the operation and manœuvres his canoe so that he can take hold of the end of the capsized craft which lies upside-down and at right angles to his cockpit. The capsized canoeist swims with his paddle to take up a position just behind the rescuer's cockpit and takes the rescuer's paddle. He reaches under the hull with one hand and then grips both gunwales of the rescuer's canoe so that his body acts as a keel to help stabilize the rescue craft (see Plate 35). The rescuer grips the end of the overturned canoe with both hands and then, in one straight pull, lifts the end and deck of the upturned canoe across his foredeck until the upturned cockpit rim is on his deck. If there is much water in the capsized canoe it will be necessary to make several pulls to achieve this position. Water will cascade out of the upturned cockpit. The rescuer now rocks the capsized canoe to empty the water completely, then quickly turns the canoe over and places the canoe alongside his own craft so that both canoes face in the same direction. The rescuer takes both paddles and rests them across the front of both cockpits. He places his nearest elbow in the cockpit of the righted craft to lock the canoes together and leans across the cockpit to grasp the far gunwale with the other hand so as to tighten the lock. The capsized canoeist moves to a position between the sterns of the two canoes, lies back in the water with his arms over the rear decks and reaches up with his feet to hook his heels over the rear of his cockpit, then prises himself up and forward into the cockpit of his canoe (see Plate 36). The rescuer retains his hold on the other canoe until the rescued canoeist has replaced his spray cover and regained his paddle from the rescuer.

In a variation of this method the capsized canoeist swims to the bows of the rescue canoe (see Plate 37). After the capsized craft has been righted, the canoe is positioned to face in the opposite direction to the rescue craft. The rescuer now reaches across the foredeck of the other canoe with his own canoe heavily tilted so that his chest is pressed hard on the deck, thus firmly stabilizing the empty craft. One hand grasps the centre of the front of the cockpit rim, the other the far gunwale. The swimmer now positions himself alongside the off-side of his own cockpit. He pulls himself, with the assistance of the rescuer who can heave on his life-jacket, across his cockpit until his chin rests on the rescuer's spray deck. His feet are still in the water (see Plate 38). He can now raise his legs, then turn and wriggle down into his cockpit. Only after the spray cover is replaced and the rescued canoeist has been handed his paddle does the rescuer release his hold on the other canoe. It should be noted that when a second rescue canoe is available this craft should raft up with the first rescue craft to give the most stable platform to effect the X rescue.

Plate 35 The X rescue method – emptying the canoe. The canoeist in the water helps stabilize the rescue craft by grasping both gunwales.

Plate 36 The X rescue method – re-entering the canoe from over the stern (see text).

Plate 37 The X rescue method (variation). As an alternative to supporting the gunwales of the rescue craft (see Plate 35), the capsized canoeist supports the bow of the rescue craft while his canoe is emptied then righted.

Plate 38 The X rescue method (variation). The capsized canoe is righted then drawn alongside the rescue craft facing in the opposite direction. The canoeist re-boards his craft over the side (see text).

Double-kayak X rescue

The X rescue method can be adapted for use with double kayaks. In this instance the capsized craft is emptied by drawing the upturned double kayak across the deck of the rescue craft between the two crewmen while the capsized crew hold the bow and stern of the rescue craft or, hold the gunwales of the rescue craft, one on either side so as to act as stabilizers. The capsized crew can then re-enter their craft from over the side or from either end using the techniques previously described.

The Eskimo Roll

The Eskimo roll is an advanced safety technique in which the canoeist corrects a capsize by using his paddle as a support to regain his position on the surface. It is a skill that once learned gives considerable added confidence to the paddler, particularly when canoeing in difficult water conditions. The roll is a development of sculling for support and its mechanics are simple (Fig. 11). After a capsize the paddle is first aligned on or just under the surface. A sculling action

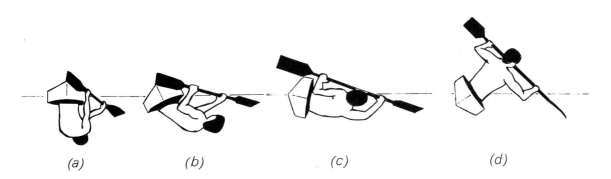

(a)   *(b)*   *(c)*   *(d)*

Fig. 11 The screw roll. (a) push the paddle up parallel to the hull and close to the surface; (b) scull the paddle just below the surface out and away from the hull; (c) continue the movement and keep the body low; (d) jerk the hips but continue the scull; if need be, scull forward to fully right the craft.

Plate 39 The screw roll. Demonstrating the starting position that is assumed under the water.

Plate 40 The screw roll. After capsizing push the paddle up with both hands so that it lies on or just under the surface.

Plate 41 The screw roll. Scull the paddle out and away from the bow and the canoe will commence to rotate upwards but the body is kept low (see Fig. 11).

enables the blade to retain its position near the surface so that any pressure exerted on the paddle by the canoeist will ensure that the canoe and occupant rotate upwards. The modern roll therefore comprises a combination of the sculling motion of the paddle, a sustained pressure on the loom followed by a hip flick to completely right the craft. The Eskimo roll is best learned in a swimming pool with one qualified instructor to each pupil. It should not be attempted by a novice without an expert readily at hand, ie standing in the water alongside the canoeist, and only then after recognized confidence and teaching stages have been satisfactorily completed. These progressive stages are given in detail in the British Canoe Union Handbook. However, it should be stressed that when properly taught the Eskimo roll is not a difficult skill for the novice to master. There are various forms of roll and it is not possible to describe them in a book of this size but the popular screw roll is outlined to give an idea of the sequence involved:

(a) Sit in the canoe with the paddle held in the normal paddle grasp. Now slide the left hand against the neck of the left blade and hold the paddle so that the left hand is just behind the hip and the paddle is parallel to the canoe.

(b) Lean forward; the backs of the hands face outboard, the spoon of the forward blade faces uppermost and is horizontal. The loom of the paddle is now twisted so that the outboard side of the fore blade is very slightly lowered (see Plate 39).

(c) Capsize, hold the lean-forward position and push the paddle up with both hands so that the paddle lies on or just under the surface (see Plate 40).

(d) Lean out from the canoe and scull the paddle out and away from the bow; the canoe will rotate upwards; the hips lead the way with the head and body low (see Plate 41).

(e) The sweep continues and the craft is almost righted. This can be achieved by a jerk of the hips, or the angle of the outboard blade can be changed and the paddle sculled forward to obtain additional purchase on the water until the upright position is reached.

Safety on Open Waters

Inland lakes can offer excellent water for canoe training, day tours and expeditions. Lake canoeing is fun and small sheltered lakes are normally safe for basic training provided that safety rules are adhered to. However, large lakes can be seriously affected by weather changes and may present conditions that can resemble the sea. Mountain lakes are particularly susceptible to sudden local squalls which, in a matter of minutes, can transform a mirror surface to a mass of short white-crested rollers that will test the skill of experienced canoeists, particularly if they are some distance off shore. The following points should therefore be noted when planning canoeing projects on large open lakes:

(a) Canoes should be of suitable design (see Fig. 2). The slalom canoe can be adapted for lake canoeing by fitting a skeg (Fig. 12) which reduces the tendency to yaw with each paddle stroke and so maintain a straighter course. Even so, the author does not recommend the slalom canoe for long-distance lake expeditions and a suitable sea design is desirable.

(b) Canoes must have adequate reserve

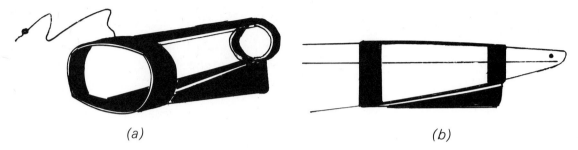

(a)   *(b)*

Fig. 12 The skeg is a form of static rudder that can be fitted to the stern section of the slalom kayak to help give directional stability and overcome the tendency to yaw. (a) The glass fibre skeg can be secured to the canoe by a retaining cord. (b) The skeg in position on the canoe.

buoyancy (see page 9) and be in good condition. A moderate leak in the hull of a canoe when on a river presents no real problem for the craft can be beached, quickly emptied and, if needs be, repaired. When on a lake a mile offshore, the same situation can be much more serious and the intake of water eventually affects the stability of the canoe.

(c) All ancillary equipment such as painters, toggles, spray covers, footrests, paddles (including spares), whistles, flares, life-jackets should be checked for serviceability.

(d) Two-stage life-jackets of the BCU-recommended type (page 17) should be worn. These will give 40 lb (18·16 kg) of buoyancy when fully inflated, are self-righting and will keep the face of an unconscious person clear of the water.

(e) Lake water can be extremely cold and therefore suitable protective clothing should be worn to combat spray conditions and, at worst, immersion in water after a capsize and bail-out.

(f) The leader, who should be adequately qualified for the position, must ensure that the party is capable of carrying out the intended plan. Particular attention should be paid to the experience, ability and strength of the individual group members. The group should be trained in rafting up (Fig. 13) and deep-water rescue procedures before an expedition commences.

(g) The group must be fully briefed on whistle signals to be used, including distress calls, and also the formation to be kept. A fairly close group is best, with the leader in the middle where he can control the party and an experienced canoeist slightly ahead to set the course.

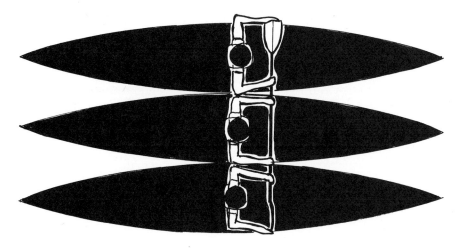

Fig. 13 Rafting up. Two or more canoeists can raft up by drawing closely alongside and firmly grasping each other's paddles to form a stable raft. The technique can be used as a safety measure when in open rough water conditions to prevent a capsize; when a leader or instructor wishes to address or instruct his group; to enable a group to rest

Plate 42 Confidence practice. Simulating rough water conditions by raising and twisting the canoe can give valuable support stroke practice and therefore greater confidence to deal with actual rough water conditions.

57

Canoeing

(h) The leader must check the local weather forecast before an expedition starts out. He should, if possible, notify a responsible person ashore of the intended route and the estimated time of arrival at the planned destination.

(i) If rough-water skills and rescue practice are being carried out in inclement weather the practice area should be carefully selected so that, in the event of a mishap, the prevailing wind and swell will quickly beach equipment and crew and not drive them offshore.

Individual Proficiency

Canoe safety also encompasses the correct instruction of the individual, his degree of proficiency in handling his canoe plus the canoeist's knowledge of safety rules and the management of his equipment. The British Canoe Union has set standards of individual proficiency that test and recognize the canoeist's skill, experience and knowledge. Appendix B gives details of the BCU Inland Proficiency Test — Kayak, and the Advanced Inland Test — Kayak. The purpose of the former test is to ensure that the canoeist can be considered safe on easy rivers and lakes under normal water conditions and is competent to handle his kayak as a member of an expedition paddling grade I rivers. The latter test is more difficult and the canoeist has to prove that he has the technical skill and experience to lead a small group of competent canoeists on a grade III river.

Canoeing has been described by some as a dangerous pursuit. Like many other outdoor activities it is often intended to be challenging and adventurous with some element of risk. However, it is not the sport of canoeing that is dangerous, it is those individuals who fail to recognize or adhere to straightforward safety procedures and rules and thus submit themselves to unnecessary risk and hazard. Therefore it is essential to know the safety rules and adhere to them.

CHAPTER FIVE

River Canoeing

Reading the Water

It is very necessary that a canoeist who intends to paddle mountain rivers can 'read' the water so as to understand how a river flows. Practical experience is essential before a river's features can be fully appreciated, but the information and advice offered in this chapter is aimed at giving important basic background knowledge about the characteristics of rivers. The canoeist who can 'read' the water can make use of the current to his advantage. He can, by studying the surface, also recognize the hazards that may lie ahead of him, on or just under the surface.

The course of a mountain river is rarely straight and the bed seldom smooth and flat. Rivers usually flow rapidly near their source and then slow gradually as they get nearer the sea, but the water always seeks out the easiest path downward. Where the river runs straight and the banks are of even height the faster current is normally in the centre. Where one bank is higher than the other the faster current is usually close to the high bank. When there is a bend in a fast-flowing mountain river the current will take the outside of the bend, which will also be the deepest part. In such regions

shallows may run out from the inner bank and strong eddies, that turn upstream, can seriously reduce a canoeist's speed if he fails to follow the main current and cuts the corner. As the river bed is rarely smooth, there are often deep and shallow spots. Boulders and rocks may protrude from the bottom so that the water forms channels. In fast water submerged obstructions are rarely visible but, if you observe carefully, the turbulence caused can be seen on the water's surface and, from the position of the turbulence, the location of the obstructions noted. By studying the river you can see the channels and the distribution of currents. Once you know which way the water runs and what is ahead, you can select the best course downstream.

Rocks and channels

Rocks are the most common hazard on a mountain river. Those which protrude above the water can be seen at a distance and are easily avoided, but those just below the surface are more difficult to locate. Rocks lying below the surface in very calm water are often almost impossible to locate, particularly when strong sunlight forms a glare on the water's surface or the water is not clear. However, a canoe draws only a few inches of water and a glass fibre hull is very durable. It is sufficiently flexible to absorb a fair impact, so running over a rock will not normally cause any real damage though it will make a fair noise. Rocks set fractionally below the surface in a rapid are a greater hazard. They can often only be located by the white aerated turbulence formed below the rock which will contrast with the smooth slower-flowing water piled on the upstream side which flows around and over the obstruction. However, if observed from downstream the obstruction can often be clearly seen. If the flow is smooth and even, a rock just below the surface may be shown up by the water creating two waves which diverge from the rock and point upstream

to the obstruction. The apex of the 'V' should therefore be avoided. When there is considerable pressure of water over a rock the water will rise up to form a pillow over the top of the obstruction, then a smooth dip which breaks up in aerated white water downstream of the rock (Fig. 14). Once you have enough experience to judge the depth of the water, and this is soon gained, many such obstructions can be paddled over. Where there are a number of rocks scattered across the river the water will be forced between the rocks. If viewed from above the channels will show as a number of 'V's' pointing downstream. The water will converge at the apex of the 'V's' to form standing waves, often with white rollers which indicate the deepest channel, free of rocks.

Fig. 14 A rock just below the surface makes a pillow of water, then a dip, followed by a white water wave.

Rapids
Where there is a distinct change in the level of the river through a sudden slope in the rock-bed, or where the river's course becomes constricted by rocks or islands or is forced into a gorge, rapids will form. Rapids can vary in type and are graded according to their difficulty (see Appendix A). Shallow rapids with regular low waves (Rough Water I) are easily negotiated and are ideal for the beginner. Long unbroken stretches of heavy rapids with high irregular waves,

submerged rocks, whirlpools and fast eddies (Rough Water V) are very difficult to run. The most difficult rapids are Rough Water VI which are highly dangerous. Rapids can be caused by:
(a) A sudden drop in the river bed forming a sloping ledge over which the river pours to create standing waves at the bottom of the descent (Fig. 15).
(b) The river becomes acutely constricted by an outcrop of rock so that most water is forced through on one side of the river (Fig. 16).

Fig. 15 Rapids formed by a sudden drop in the river bed.

BANK

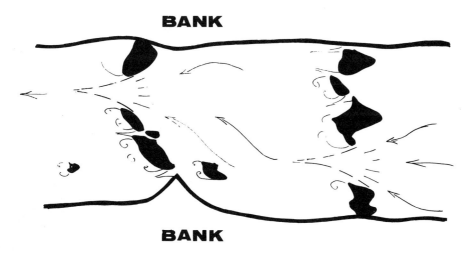

BANK

Fig. 16 Rapids formed by outcrops of rock constricting the main flow.

Fig. 17 Rapids formed by rock ledges under the river's surface.

(c) The channel becomes constricted by rocks on and below the surface so that turbulence and waves form.

(d) Fast water runs down a slope on to patches or areas of calm water. The fast water is forced back to curl over and form 'stopper' waves.

(e) Rock ledges in a descending river bed creating considerable turbulence. If there is a fast current and the river is reasonably shallow, standing waves will form downstream of each ledge. (Fig. 17).

(f) Reeds under the surface causing waves which, unlike other river waves, may move from side to side brought about by the swaying of the reeds.

Technique

Small waves present little difficulty to a canoeist. Larger waves known as 'haystacks' are found at the point of the 'V' of a rapid and can stand well up out of the water with a tumbling white head. These need to be tackled with care. Where a large mass of fast water runs onto smooth water, a 'stopper' will form that tumbles over and over on itself. When negotiating large haystacks and stopper waves the canoeist must drive the canoe through the surging mass of water. Large wide rapids move fast and as most obstructions are well below the surface, cross-currents and waves are the main problem. It is therefore important to keep up forward speed and not allow the craft to drift, for unless the speed of the canoe is above that of the current it can prove difficult to control the kayak. Remember that the most stable way of negotiating any standing wave is to drive the canoe through it.

Eddies are currents which turn and flow upstream. They are caused by obstructions on and below the surface such as rocks, bridge piers and changes in the contour of the river bank. The current in an eddy often flows in a circle; slow water in the middle and fast water on the outside. Once the bow of a canoe is caught in an eddy the craft can be pulled out of the main current. However, strong eddies behind rocks can often be spotted well in advance and used as a resting point into which to turn before negotiating the remainder of a rapid.

The following principles, techniques and strokes are applicable when running mountain rivers.

Inspecting rapids
Unless you are sure that a rapid ahead is straightforward and within your capability of running safely, always stop upstream of the rapid, get out, then walk along the bank to observe the water from both above and below the rapid. Seek out the best course down the rapid and note the exact position of obstructions. Fallen trees are dangerous obstructions and should be kept well clear of, for an unwary canoeist could be swept under the branches and trapped. Note the best point of entry into the rapid and where, if

necessary, it may be possible to turn into an eddy to rest and await the arrival of your companions or perhaps practise your high telemark and re-entry techniques.

Avoiding obstructions
Obstructions ahead can be avoided by using the high moving draw stroke interspersed with normal paddle strokes. Take note that when each draw stroke is almost completed and the paddle drawn near the hull, the blade is then turned to pull through as in the normal paddle stroke so as not to interrupt the paddle rhythm. A very effective technique for avoiding obstructions is known as the ferry glide which enables the canoeist to cross the current and position himself where he wants to be without being swept downstream (Fig. 18). It is a technique that can soon be learned and

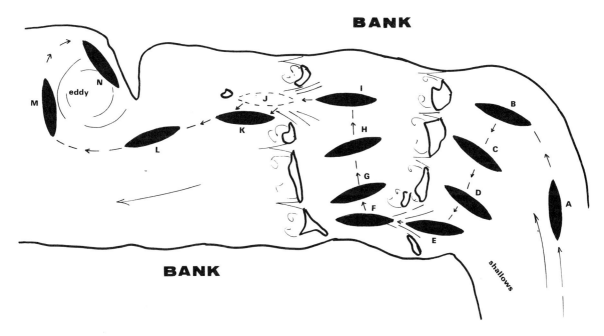

Fig. 18 River technique. (A) The canoeist follows the main current which runs on the outside of the bend but has to immediately back-paddle to ferry glide his craft to port (B)–(E), then to starboard (F)–(I) in order to take the correct channels. At (J) he makes a moving draw stroke to port and position (K) in order to miss the rock ahead, then turns in the eddy to await the rest of the party (M and N).

Canoeing

should be practised where the flow is 3 mph (5 kpm) or more so that the canoe can be effectively moved sideways, pushed by the water pressure against its side. The help given by the current is appreciated more easily if at first the canoeist faces upstream. Line the craft up with an object on each bank, perhaps a branch or stone. If the fastest current is in the centre of the river, point the bow slightly across the current towards the other bank and paddle forward to hold the boat in position against the current.

As the current is weak near the bank, the angle of the canoe to the flow may be fairly wide. When the centre of the river is reached, the current becomes stronger and the angle of the canoe is reduced – otherwise the fast water will push the craft downstream. The paddler should continually check his position in relation to the objects he has selected on the bank, so that he neither moves upstream nor drifts downstream. If the angle becomes too wide and the canoe commences to broach, correct the turn

Plate 43 Entering a grade I rapid. Rocks ahead to the left of the canoeist will require him to ferry glide the craft to his right (see Plate 44).

Plate 44 By back-paddling with the stern of the canoe across to his right, the canoeist ferry glides to clear the obstruction (see Fig. 18).

with a stern rudder or reverse sweep stroke on the opposite side of the turn. Once the principle of the ferry glide has been learned facing upstream, turn the canoe around and practise the technique facing downstream so that you are able to hold the craft against the current by back-paddling and can move the canoe across the river from side to side at will.

Turning
To turn quickly out of a fast current use the telemark technique (see Plate 18). If turning into an eddy use the high telemark (see Plates 19 and 20).

Support strokes
When in rough water, the canoeist can obtain considerable stability from his paddle. Even simple strokes carry a stabilizing component, for while the paddle is on or under the surface, purchase is afforded by the water. Paddle braces are those strokes designed to give

maximum stability. The low brace resembles a low telemark without the strong lean and with the paddle further out from the stern. The low brace can be applied on either side and can alternate with normal paddle strokes so as to keep up speed (see Plate 50 for the double kayak brace). The high brace is a more aggressive stroke and is used in very turbulent water. The canoeist places his paddle deep through the light top layer of aerated water in order to obtain support from the calmer stable flow below. The lower hand is held in the water so as to push the blade deep. The stroke can be used with or without a lean (Fig. 19).

Entering fast water
When entering fast water in order to proceed down river from a calm area such as a bay in the river bank or from behind a large rock or bridge pier, the

Plate 45 Demonstrating a high brace in a fast run of water (see Fig. 19).

Fig. 19 The high brace is a support stroke used in deep turbulent water. If the paddle is placed deep on the left side of the canoe, as shown, its stabilizing effect will also prevent a capsize to the right.

force of the current can be used to support the canoeist. Face across the current and slightly upstream, then paddle hard to break out from the eddy. As you do so, raise the paddle to a stationary high draw position and lean downstream onto the paddle so that the upstream gunwale is raised. The water pressure will support the paddle and the canoeist (Fig. 20). The faster the water, the greater should be the lean. If you don't lean sufficiently, the water will build up on the upstream gunwale and deck and tip you in on that side. Once the kayak has been turned downstream by the current, sit up and paddle away.

Running aground and portaging
Where the river bed shelves suddenly to shallow water and there is no available

Plate 46 Entering fast water from an eddy. Lean downstream and the current will give support to the paddle. The faster the water, the greater should be the lean (see Fig. 20).

Fig. 20 Entering fast water, lean away from the current onto the paddle. The pressure of the water under the blade will support you and the current cannot build up on the upstream gunwale and tip you in (see also Plate 46).

deep channel to take, a canoe may run aground and be held firmly. If the canoe has broached across the current, get out of the canoe (see Method 3, page 24) on the upstream side and immediately grasp the now lightened craft. If you get out of the canoe on the downstream side, the force of the water will press the canoe against you and could well push you over. If a double canoe runs aground facing downstream, the sternman should disembark quickly from the canoe then hold the stern while the bowman gets out. If the craft broaches as it grounds, both the crew need to get out on the upstream side of the canoe. The canoe can now be lined down the shallows; that is, the painter undone and held so

Canoeing

that the lightened craft floats down the shallow water while the canoeist(s) wade behind (see Plate 52). It may at times be necessary to portage around obstructions such as weirs, falls, dangerous rapids or fallen trees (see Plate 51).

To re-board the single kayak in mid-channel from water about knee deep, use the technique shown in Method 4 (see page 23). In order to set off in a double canoe from mid-stream facing down river, the sternman will get in first while the bowman holds the stern. Once aboard and with the spray cover fitted, the sternman holds the canoe in position by back-paddling while the bowman boards.

Should the canoe become stuck on a rock in a fast run of water or rapid and turn broadside, immediately lean downstream against the rock, as the force of the water under the hull will tend to lift the canoe and help you free the craft (Fig. 21). If you don't lean, the water will build up on the gunwale and deck then quickly tip you in on the upstream side (Fig. 22). It may be necessary to push on the rock with the paddle or hand in order to free the craft. Should the current catch the stern you will continue your journey, but backwards! However, you are now in your strongest position to hold the craft against the current. By paddling forward and observing the current and rocks below, you can ferry glide (see page 63) the craft into an eddy then, when ready, re-enter the current (see Plate 46) and paddle on down river.

Fig. 21 If you broadside on to a rock lean downstream and the current will tend to lift the hull so that you can push off the obstruction (see Fig. 22).

Fig. 22. If you broadside on to a rock and don't lean downstream the current will immediately build up on your gunwale and tip you in.

CHAPTER SIX

Planning a River Expedition

A river-canoeing expedition can give great enjoyment. It is possible to paddle with comparative ease through remote and beautiful country, yet have sufficient supplies and equipment on board to set up a comfortable camp each night. There is much to see on a mountain river; the flight of wild duck overhead, the long-legged heron perched on rocks in midstream, the leaping salmon that can at times almost land on your deck. The days can be exciting, with each person applying his individual skills to meet the challenge of fast water and rapids. At night a small fire of driftwood can be lit on a shingle beach and supper barbecued before retiring for a well-deserved sleep. However, to get maximum enjoyment from a river expedition there needs to be sound planning and good organization. Various factors have to be considered when a river tour is planned, such as the degree of proficiency of the party, the grading of the river, the type of equipment available, time available for the tour and, most important, the experience of the leader.

Basic Planning

The first factor to consider is the selection of a suitable river. The degree of difficulty of rivers may differ according to the international system of grading rivers (see Appendix A). A river that is graded as RW/WW I is eminently suited for a beginners' expedition as it will have sufficiently exciting water to provide novices with a challenge but without undue risk. Even so, the expedition should be planned and led by an experienced leader and the group itself will require training beforehand.

The second factor to consider is the type of equipment available. Lath and canvas designs are suitable for deep waterways and canals but are not really ideal for mountain rivers which often have fast shallows, pebble banks and hidden rocks. The amount of damage a rubberized-fabric-covered hull can withstand is much less than the tougher and more durable glass-fibre hull. Consider also the size of the craft to be used and the space available for the storage of kit. The amount of gear that can be stowed in a slalom design is normally less than that which will fit into a 14 ft 6 in (442 cm) single-seat tourer. The number of stops planned en route to take on supplies may therefore depend on the amount of stowage space available and, when using a canoe with limited carrying capacity, it may be necessary to have frequent stops, perhaps every other day.

A third factor that must be considered is the ability of the party, with particular reference to the weaker members. The degree of difficulty to be expected must be within the ability of the less able members unless the project is well supported and organized for training purposes. The length of each day's paddle should also depend on the strength of the weaker paddlers. A good average day's paddle on a mountain river with a fair current is about 15 to 20 miles (24 to 32 km). This allows for time to inspect rapids, for portages, rest periods to brew up a hot drink on the bank, as well as time for breaking camp each morning, packing and stowing, and also for making camp at night. It is far better to under-estimate when planning distance than to over-estimate. To have extra time to relax in the evening by a camp fire after a good meal is much more enjoyable than having to set up camp as darkness is falling with everyone tired and with the knowledge that you must break camp at first light to keep to the schedule planned.

Always check that you have the right or permission to canoe on water. In many countries, and particularly so in remote areas, a canoeist can paddle his canoe just about wherever he pleases. However, on some comparatively narrow but valuable fishing rivers such as exist in Great Britain care must be taken not to offend riparian owners. In Great Britain you have a right to canoe on any part of a river that is subject to the rise and fall of the tide, but above the tide limit no further right may exist unless it is dedicated by act of Parliament as in the case of the rivers Thames, Severn and the Wye below Glasbury. On some rivers fishermen do not object to canoeists, but on others permission must be sought before canoeing may take place. It is most important that good relations exist between fishermen and canoeists so, if in doubt, seek advice from your national canoe organization; in the case of Britain, the British Canoe Union. (See Appendix C.)

Leader's Responsibility
In many ways the task of organizing a river expedition for novices or canoeists of limited experience sets greater demands on the leader than organizing an advanced expedition made up of experienced canoeists. Good leadership is very important. The responsibilities of the leader of a canoe expedition are numerous and varied. It is not a position to be offered nor accepted lightly, for a good leader has qualities over and above experience and technical skill. He should be a level-headed person who possesses suitable attributes of character, such as determination, and coolness in adversity, and is able to stimulate his group under conditions of both sun and spate. Correct leadership encompasses the ability to communicate and act clearly, a continual appreciation of the progress of a group and an acute awareness of the necessity not to undertake any challenge that is beyond the ability of the group. There is no complete code of rules that a leader should follow in order to cover every possible eventuality that may be experienced, but the leader's

responsibilities will involve him in individual and group safety, the sound control of the party when on the river and possibly in basic planning. The following pre-expedition checks and river briefing will serve as a sound basis for a leader to follow, whether the project is to be a straightforward three-day tour or a lengthy major expedition.

Pre-expedition checks
Prior to the expedition commencing the leader should:
(a) Ensure that he has full knowledge of the river with adequate river guides that give a complete itinerary of the river and also maps for himself and the group.
(b) Satisfy himself that the project is within the ability of his group unless difficult areas of a river are to be portaged or the expedition is to be an adequately supported training venture.
(c) Satisfy himself that his assistants have sufficient experience and are fully proficient in the administering of artificial respiration.
(d) Confirm that adequate transport arrangements exist for personnel and equipment to and from the river.
(e) Unless the expedition is a wilderness trip, select and arrange camp sites before hand.
(f) If the requirement exists, arrange clearance at set points for access to and from the river.
(g) Have an emergency plan to evacuate a sick or injured person should such illness or accident arise.
(h) If equipment is to be self-provided, make sure that all group members have a check list of personal, camping and canoeing equipment required.
(i) Ensure that all group members know the outline plans of the project including their duties, the dates, times of start and finish, distances planned, references of campsites etc.
(j) Ensure that unfamiliar and new equipment is thoroughly tested.
(k) Personally inspect the canoes and life-jackets of novices to ensure that all are in order and that each canoeist is familiar with the correct usage of his equipment.
(l) Ensure that he and his assistant(s) will carry emergency equipment comprising spare paddles, a 50 ft rescue rope (kept in a bag), a short tow rope and a first aid kit.

River briefing
Before the paddle commences, the leader should brief his group. If the expedition is to comprise several days, periodic briefings are necessary. The briefing should be based on the following, but amended or amplified as circumstances demand. The leader should:
(a) Outline group plans for the day and note on maps the position of hazards. He should revise the whistle signals to be used by the leader and his assistant(s). If manual signals are to be used re-demonstrate these, eg paddle of lead canoeist held up with arms straight = stop; paddle extended towards bank = pull into side; paddle held vertical = clear to run down rapid, etc.
(b) Re-cap on the organization of the group. Emphasize that the party will keep compact and not string out; the lead canoe will be paddled by an experienced canoeist: the rear canoeist will have special responsibility for rescue; each canoeist is responsible for the craft behind him; all must be observant, look out for rocks and

Canoeing

hazards and indicate these to the craft behind, then see that craft safely past the hazard.

(c) Give the position of each canoeist in the single-file formation to be used. The slowest paddlers are allocated places near the front of the party so that they cannot straggle behind.

(d) Outline clearly the procedure to adopt when encountering a rapid. The group will stop well clear of the rapid and, if necessary, get out and inspect from both above and below the rapid in order to select the best course down river. They will then descend the rapid singly and wait in the slack water below for the group to re-assemble. Signals to control the descent of the group should be re-capped.

(e) State the position the leader will take. He may wish to take up a position in the middle of the file so that he can observe what is going on both ahead and behind him. He may, on the other hand, wish to maintain a roving position.

(f) Revise what action to take in the event of a capsize and also re-cap on basic safety rules.

(g) Finally stress that in the interest of safety his decisions are final.

It should be noted that one person cannot supervise more than eight canoes, therefore where large canoeing projects are planned the leader will require suitably qualified assistants to control groups of canoeists.

Canoe Camping

The touring canoeist is not limited to the same relatively small amount of equipment a hiker can carry. Most canoes perform well with a fair weight on board if packed and loaded properly,

Plate 47 A river expedition. Planning the day's paddle and checking the river's features with the aid of a map and river guide.

and the extra load is hardly felt by the paddler. It is possible to pack aboard a touring design sufficient stores to last several days plus all the camping and personal equipment needed. However, don't take items that are not essential. If you have to portage at rapids or a weir, then what has been put into the canoe has to be taken out and physically carried, perhaps some distance. Neither is there any point in duplicating equipment if only one item is needed. Two people can share one tent, two or three people one stove. One suitably sized canteen set can also be shared. Take along items that are dual purpose. A rubberized or canvas sheet will serve, when afloat, to protect tins of food if properly folded and tied. At camp it can be converted into a cooking shelter with the aid of paddles or driftwood branches and string to support the cover. A gallon heat-resistant tin-can securely covered with a piece of water-proofed fabric will serve, when afloat, as a container for perishable food. At camp it can be used as a water carrier or a brew-can which in bad weather can be kept simmering over an open fire on the shingle so that a hot drink is readily available.

General items

A list of general items of equipment required for a canoe camping expedition is as follows:

Life-jacket (should be in first-class condition and preferably be of the BCU-recommended type)
Tent, poles and pegs
Groundsheet, if not built into tent
Sleeping bag(s)
Stove
Fuel
Tin frying pan and saucepan or canteen set
Tin kettle
Knife, fork and spoon
Tin opener
Plate and soup bowl
1 pint mug (polythene)
Tupperware or similar airtight containers (for carrying sugar, tea, fresh milk, etc)
Pocket knife, with saw blade and corkscrew
Sun glasses
Small axe (one between a group of about 6 people)
Waterproof bags (rubberized-fabric inner bags and large canvas outer bags)
Trowel (for disposal of waste)
Brillo pads (for cleaning pans or mess tins)
Matches in waterproof containers
Toilet paper
Toilet requisites
First aid kit
Helazone tablets (for purifying water)
1-inch-to-the-mile map and river guide (sealed in a clean polythene envelope)
Thermos (best protected in a canvas bag of similar shape and tied inside the cockpit)
Waterproof torch (with spare battery and bulb)

Packing and loading

A certain amount of water will get into a canoe. It will drain off your shoes after you have boarded from shallow water. It may seep in through the minute gap between the spray cover and the cockpit coaming when the canoe is run through standing waves and the deck is awash. In the event of a capsize in rough water the hull of a canoe may take in a considerable amount of water. It is therefore extremely important that all items of personal equipment, camping equipment and food which could be spoiled (such as clothes, sleeping bags, tents and perishable food stuffs) are well packed in waterproof bags. Other items such as cooking gear, eating utensils and canned food are placed in bags or suitable containers and not allowed to roll around loose in the hull. In order to obtain maximum protection it is often best to put items in a small waterproof bag and then pack several such bags inside a larger canvas waterproof bag which is well sealed. In the event of a capsize, the air trapped in these bags will give extra buoyancy to the canoe. Though there may be a fair amount of room in a canoe, items need to be packed in a tidy fashion so check in advance of the expedition that packages will fit conveniently into the hull. It is best to make this check at home, perhaps on the lawn or garage floor. Gather all your gear around the canoe – tent, sleeping bag, stove, utensils, spare clothes, food, etc. Look carefully at the space available within the bow and stern sections, then plan what will go where (Fig. 23).

There is no real set order of stowing gear, but if the tent can be packed in a reasonably accessible position so much the better. In the event of heavy rain it can be taken out and erected first, then other items can be removed from the protection of the hull and unpacked in the tent. Items that will be needed on the journey such as the Thermos, stove, repair kit, sun glasses, sweets, food for a mid-day break, sweater or anorak should be stowed within easy reach of the cockpit. If possible, tie packages to frame members so that in the event of a capsize they cannot float out. However, make sure that there are no loose lines that can get caught up with your feet and that your leg room is not restricted in any way. When setting off on an expedition the canoe can normally be loaded on the bank and then, with one person at either end, lowered gently onto the water.

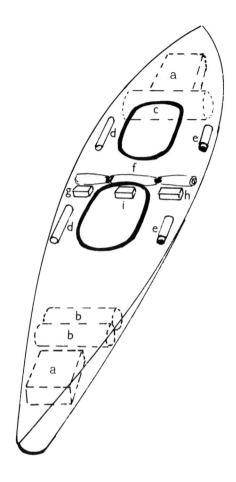

Fig. 23 Packing a double kayak for a river expedition. (a) stores and clothes; (b) sleeping bags; (c) tent; (d) spare clothing and anoraks; (e) Thermos; (f) bivouac sheet; (g) stove; (h) food for the day; (i) cooking utensils.

However, if the canoe is to be heavily loaded it may be necessary to load the craft on the water for it could be difficult to lift and the frame of a lath and canvas design could be strained when loaded unsupported on the bank. When fully laden with all equipment, stores and the crew is aboard, the canoe should float level on the water or be slightly down at the stern. If long stretches of open water are to be covered in a fair wind (and areas of a river can be very exposed), it may be necessary to re-adjust the load. If there is a strong following wind, trim the canoe by the stern so that the stern lies deeper in the water and is not blown to one side. Similarly, if there is a strong head wind, add more weight to the bow section so that the bow will hold its position.

Plate 48 Loading the canoe. All equipment is well packed in waterproof bags then stored securely in the hull.

Plate 49 Setting off. The sternman holds the canoe into the current while the bowman gets in and secures the spray cover.

Plate 50 Under way. The commencement of a grade II rapid demonstrating low brace strokes.

Plate 51 Hazards en route. Portaging around fallen trees.

Plate 52 Lining down shallows, often met with on grade I mountain river expeditions.

Plate 53 If in doubt, get out of the canoe and check unfamiliar rapids from above and below.

Plate 54 An exciting part of the expedition – running a grade II rapid.

Selecting a camp site

In remote areas it is often possible to camp at any suitable site for there may not be any restrictions on camping. This makes for flexible planning. If therefore the weather is good, the current strong and the wind favourable, the party may find that they are still fresh at the end of the day and have the energy and time to paddle a further 5 miles (8 km) or so. Bad weather conditions on the other hand can force a halt to the day's canoeing activities before the intended distance has been covered. Amendments to the original programme may therefore not pose difficulties in finding a campsite in the wilds, but when planning canoe expeditions in less isolated settings different plans should be made. A series of alternative sites agreed by the landowners beforehand and, if possible, inspected, can give flexibility to original schedules and allow for necessary reductions or increases in the distances planned. Whatever distance is to be covered, plan to set up camp at least three hours before sunset so as to give sufficient time to erect tents and shelters then make a meal before the night sets in.

Plate 55 Setting up camp.

Canoeing

The following points need to be noted when selecting a camp site:

(a) The site should be level, clear of overhanging trees and branches which can hinder movement and drip onto canvas long after a rain storm has passed. Avoid areas with thistles and nettles; they also harbour insects.

(b) Avoid low areas that are liable to flood and check the height of previous floods from the high-water marks on rocks and also the height of driftwood debris. A flash flood caused by a local but severe storm many miles upstream can cause serious problems lower down the river, particularly if the river narrows into a gorge, which will force the water to rise dramatically. Therefore don't camp on sandy beaches in a gorge however attractive the site may be, for even with an escape path you could loose your tent, equipment and canoe.

(c) Avoid slippery, steep, muddy banks, for after a rain shower you will have great difficulty in getting your canoe back down the bank. Packing the craft on the slippery surface may be a rather perilous operation and getting in might prove difficult.

(d) Low-lying sites can be plagued with insects such as midges and mosquitoes, particularly if the site is near rushes or a backwater. A higher elevation is often exposed to a breeze and has fewer insects.

(e) Mist often forms on the water in the early hours and if tents are erected close to the river they can still be enveloped in mist long after the early morning sun has burned off the damp vapour a few feet higher up the slope. Normally a site about 25 ft (7.50 m) above the water's surface will suffice.

(f) Camp away from and, if possible, upstream of any cattle watering places and fords.

(g) Camp if possible where the river runs clear. The freshest water is where there is a fair current.

Camp fires

A knowledge of basic fire-craft is a useful asset to the touring canoeist. A camp fire can serve to warm the party at night, dry out wet clothes after a capsize and, if constructed for the purpose, also serve to cook meals or keep a hot drink or soup simmering without using valuable gas or liquid fuel. To make a camp fire, select a safe spot clear of undergrowth and overhanging trees. A sandy cove is a good place to build a fire as no damage can be done to turf and water is close at hand to control the blaze. First of all, lay three small sticks of about 6 in (15 cm) on the ground to form a triangle with a quantity of tinder lying loosely within the centre of the triangle. The stick on the windward side rests on the top of the two other sticks to allow air to reach the centre of the tinder (Fig. 24). Light the tinder on this side of the triangle and, as it catches, add light dry kindling bit by bit to form a small pyramid over the blaze which soon completely ignites. Now add firewood to form a teepee fire which will burn cheerfully (Fig. 25). If the fire is to be continued as a tepee fire keep it small for a large one can burn too quickly and throw off too much heat for comfort. However, the small tepee fire can be developed in to a 'Star' or 'Lazy Man's' fire by adding long timbers that radiate from the centre of the blaze like the spokes of a wheel (Fig. 26). This is an

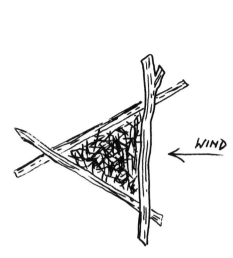

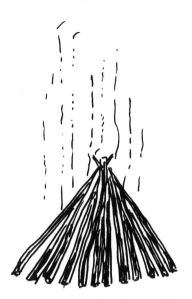

Fig. 24 Basic firelay shown from above. The tinder is contained within the triangle of sticks with the raised stick placed on the windward side.

Fig. 25 The teepee fire is suitable as a small camp fire and will blaze cheerfully.

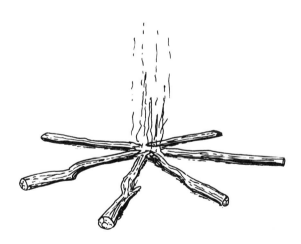

Fig. 26 The 'Star' or 'Lazyman's' fire uses little wood and requires little attention.

economical, easily controlled fire as it burns only at the ends where the timbers almost meet.

Shelters
As previously explained, a large sheet of light canvas, proofed cotton fabric or rubberized material can be of dual purpose. By day it can be folded carefully, wrapped around items of equipment and lashed securely to make a convenient parcel for storage in the hull. By night it can, with the aid of paddles or driftwood branches as supports, serve to improve the comfort of your camp and form a windshield, cooking shelter or even a bivouac in which it is possible to sleep. (See Fig. 27 a–c.)

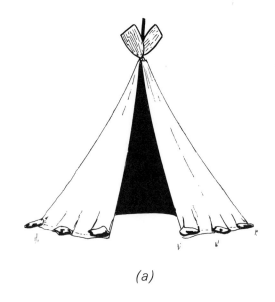

(a)

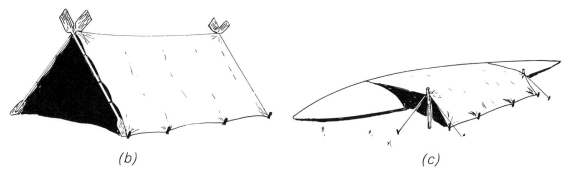

(b) *(c)*

Fig. 27 A bivouac sheet can, with the use of paddles or sticks and string, make (a) a small cooking shelter; (b) a small bivouac tent; or (c) a low bivouac sleeping shelter.

Camp organization
A canoe camp that is well organized is normally the most comfortable and enjoyable. If the project comprises a large number of people, the leader should divide the party into groups of six to eight persons each with a group leader whose task is to liaise with the over-all leader and allocate simple but essential tasks such as erecting tents, getting water, collecting driftwood for a fire and constructing a cooking shelter. Other tasks may be making a fire, cooking supper, drying clothes and then making all equipment secure for the night. It is essential that the Country Code is strictly observed and the camp is well run with proper hygienic standards. It is not

possible in a book of this size to deal in detail with the camping techniques required but the reader will find a wealth of information in *Beginner's Guide to Light-Weight Camping* (by the same author) published by Pelham Books.

Enjoyment

The degree of enjoyment to be obtained from a canoe project is a very important point to consider when planning an expedition. The project needs to be interesting and a challenge but without overtaxing the group or introducing poor standards of comfort. In bad weather, stops should be made in sheltered areas to put on extra clothing if needed, and to have a warm drink. Periodic halts should be called to allow the members to stretch legs and perhaps brew up on the bank or at the water's edge. If mishaps occur, quick action is needed so that people do not get cold or others kept waiting.

Good organization when ashore and on the water makes for more time to paddle and enjoy the adventure. That is what canoeing is all about.

International System of Grading Rivers According to Difficulty

Rough Water (RW or WW)

I Easy. Occasional small rapids, waves regular and low. Correct course easy to find, but care is needed with obstacles like pebble banks, protective works, fallen trees, etc, especially on narrow rivers.

II Medium. Fairly frequent rapids, usually with regular waves, easy eddies, or whirlpools. Course generally easy to recognize. (On the Continent: easy and medium raft channels.)

III Difficult. Rapids numerous, and with fairly high, irregular waves, broken water, eddies and whirlpools. Course not always easily recognizable. (Difficult raft channels.)

IV Very difficult. Long and extended stretches of rapids with high irregular waves, difficult broken water, eddies and whirlpools. Course often difficult to recognize. Inspection from the bank nearly always necessary. (Very difficult raft channels.)

V Exceedingly difficult. Long unbroken stretches of rapids with difficult and completely irregular broken water, submerged rocks, very difficult whirlpools and very fast eddies. Previous inspection absolutely essential.

VI The absolute limit of difficulty. All previously mentioned difficulties increased to the limit of practicability. Cannot be attempted without risk to life.

Notes on Grading

1 If a particular length of river falls between two of the above grades, or alternates between a lower and a higher grade, and portaging round the more difficult parts would not make a continuation of the trip worth while, two numbers are used, e.g. II–III.

2 If a length of river offers at one or two individual points (where a portage is easy) difficulties beyond its average grading, the higher grade of difficulty is shown as an index figure, eg II_4.

3 A rise or fall in water level always alters a river's appearance and the rating of the stretch in question, and may make it easier or quite impracticable in difficulty. The grading given is as far as possible that for 'favourable' water conditions.

APPENDIX B

BCU Proficiency Tests

Inland Proficiency Test (including open lakes) – Kayak

NOTE: The purpose of this test is to ensure that a successful candidate can be considered reasonably safe under normal water conditions. It is strongly recommended that candidates gain good practical experience of the procedures and skills required before they enter.

The candidate must satisfy the examiner that he is competent to handle his kayak safely as a member of a group touring on grade I water. The test will be taken in a single kayak, on water with a simple 2 mph current if at all possible. Where these conditions are not available, the examiner will, at his discretion, include extra tests or questions to satisfy himself that the candidate could handle his kayak on such water. The test will not be taken in a swimming pool.

The candidate will:

1 Present himself suitably equipped for the test.

2 Present for inspection the following items, which must be both suitable and serviceable:
(a) Kayak, paddle and spray cover;
(b) Bow and stern toggles and/or safety lines and/or painters;
(c) Buoyancy;
(d) Life-jacket or buoyancy aid;
(e) Repair kit and simple first aid kit;
(f) Waterproof kitbag(s).

3 Pack his waterproof kitbag(s) with the necessary items for a day's tour and stow it (them) in the kayak.

4 Demonstrate:
(a) Launching and embarking;
(b) Efficient paddling technique, forwards and backwards;
(c) Turning and coming alongside bank;
(d) Emergency stops, forwards and backwards;
(e) Drawing the kayak sideways in both directions;
(f) A support stroke on both sides;
(g) Disembarking and bringing the kayak ashore.

5 Satisfy the examiner that he can:
(a) Ferry glide, facing both upstream and downstream;
(b) Break out of or into faster current;
(c) Negotiate bends where the current sets under the trees.

6 Perform capsize drill, followed by a deep water rescue with partners. He will take charge of a rescue and then act as a capsized patient.

7 Capsize again, at least 10 metres from the landing place, bring his loaded kayak

Canoeing

to the bank and empty out the water.

8 Prove that he can swim. He will then swim 50 metres in canoeing clothing (wet or dry suits are permitted) and a fully inflated life-jacket or a buoyancy aid.

9 Answer questions on:
   (a) His practical experience, giving evidence of his having taken part in at least three one-day expeditions by kayak;
   (b) Safety;
   (c) Loading a kayak with full camping equipment;
   (d) Repairs;
   (e) The BCU River Advisory Service, and the legal position on access;
   (f) Access to local waters.

Advanced Inland Test – Kayak

The candidate must satisfy the examiner that he is able to lead a small group of competent canoeists on a grade III river. He must show that he has good practical experience at this standard and already holds the Inland Kayak Proficiency Certificate. He must have a good general knowledge of canoeing; he should have made at least four journeys of an advanced nature in a kayak and have assisted in the leadership of two of these.

The test will be taken in a single kayak, usually over a stretch of grade III water. The candidate will produce the qualifying Proficiency Certificate at the time of the test.

The candidate will:

1 Present himself suitably equipped for the test.

2 Carry out a suitable practical canoeing test, determined by the examiner.

3 Demonstrate effectively all normal strokes for handling the kayak in rough water with, against and across current.

4 Perform a first-time Eskimo roll.

5 Answer questions on:
   (a) Safety and expedition planning and leadership;
   (b) The international river grading system;
   (c) Canal and estuary canoeing;
   (d) Repairs and maintenance;
   (e) Types of canoe and equipment;
   (f) General canoeing knowledge, including competition.

APPENDIX C

National Canoe Federations

AUSTRALIA – Australian Canoe
Association
c/o Phil Coles, Box A 98 Post Office,
Sidney South 2000

AUSTRIA – Österreichischer Paddel-Sport
Verband
Berggasse 16, Wein IX

BELGIUM – Fédération Belge de Canoe
c/o A. Vandeput, Geerdegemwaart 79, B.
2800 Mechelen

CANADA – Canadian Canoe Association
333 River Road, Place Vanier, Vanier
City, Ontario K1L 8B9

DENMARK – Dansk Kano og Kajak
Forbund
c/o J. Cronberg, Engvej 184–2300
Copenhagen S

FINLAND – Suomen Kanoottiliitto ry
Topeliuksenkatu 41a, 00250 Helsinki 25

FRANCE – Fédération Française de
Canoe-Kayak
87 Quai de la Marne, 94 Joinville le
Pont

GERMAN DEMOCRATIC REPUBLIC –
Deutscher Kanu-Sport-Verband
Storkowerstr. 118, 1055 Berlin

FEDERAL REPUBLIC OF GERMANY –
Deutscher Kanu-Verband
Berta-Allee 8, 41 Duisburg

GREAT BRITAIN – British Canoe Union

70 Brompton Road, London SW3 1DT

IRELAND – Irish Canoe Union
c/o Venture Sports, Rock Hill, Blackrock,
Co Dublin

ITALY – Federazione Italiana Canottaggio
Viale Tiziano 70, 00100 Roma

LUXEMBOURG – Fédération
Luxembourgeoise de Canoe-Kayak
Boîte postale 424, Luxembourg 2

NETHERLANDS – Nederlandse Kano Bond
c/o E. H. Meulen, J. Henry Dunantstraat
62, Krommenie

NEW ZEALAND – New Zealand Canoeing
Association Inc.
P.O. Box 5125, Auckland

NORWAY – Norges Kajak-Forbund
Hauger Skolovei 1, N. 1346 Gjettum

POLAND – Polski Zwiazek Kajakowy
ul. Sienkiwicza 12, Warszawa

RUMANIA – Federatia Româna de Caiac-
Canoe
Str. Vasilo Conta 16, Bucarest

SOUTH AFRICA – South African Canoe
Association
c/o W. F. van Riet, 13 Leipold Street,
Bellville

SPAIN – Federacion Espagnola de
Piragüismo
Cea Bermudez 14 3°, DP. 10–11
Madrid 3

Canoeing

SWEDEN – Svenska Kanotförbundet
Svenska Kanotförbundet
Stockholm
SWITZERLAND – Schweizerischer Kanu-
Verband
c/o Kamber, Gundeldingerrain 187, 4059
Basle
U.S.A. – American Canoe Association

c/o Commodore A. C. A. Lawrence E.
Zuk, 189 Prairie Str. Concord, Mass.
01742
YUGOSLAVIA – Kajakaski-Savez
Jugoslavije
Bulevar Revolucije 44/I, 1100
Beograd